TAKE CHARGE!

A Woman's Guide
to a Secure Retirement

by Edie Milligan, CFP, AFC, CW

ALPHA

A Pearson Education Company

Copyright © 2002 by Edie Milligan

International Standard Book Number: 0-02-864195-7
Library of Congress Catalog Card Number: 2001094728

04   03   02   8   7   6   5   4   3   2   1

Interpretation of the printing code: The rightmost number of the first series of numbers is the year of the book's printing; the rightmost number of the second series of numbers is the number of the book's printing. For example, a printing code of 02-1 shows that the first printing occurred in 2002.

Printed in the United States of America

Publisher: *Marie Butler-Knight*
Product Manager: *Phil Kitchel*
Managing Editor: *Jennifer Chisholm*
Acquisitions Editor: *Mike Sanders*
Development Editor: *Tom Stevens*
Production Editor: *Katherin Bidwell*
Copy Editor: *Cari Luna*
Cover Designer: *Doug Wilkins*
Book Designer: *Trina Wurst*
Indexer: *Tonya Heard*
Layout/Proofreading: *Mary Hunt, Michelle Mitchell*
Managing Project Director: *Joseph Roberts*

Contents

Introduction

Mary Elizabeth Milligan was the real writer in the family. Last Thanksgiving, at the age of 45, breast cancer took her life. She didn't make it to retirement.

Beth was my big cousin, three years my senior. She got to wear fishnet hose while I was still wearing bobby socks. I didn't have a big sister, so she was it.

She always encouraged me to write. But she was a great writer and I couldn't see myself as ever being that good. This book is the start of me "givin' it a shot."

We've all known and loved women who have been taken by breast cancer. Fewer and fewer are dying, thankfully, than in past years. Those of us who escape this devastating disease and other causes of early death have a tremendous challenge: to be responsible for our own futures.

The pressures and complexities of life in the twenty-first century make it hard enough to be responsible for today, let alone tomorrow. But, life has always been hard for women, and we are making strides every day in our quest for economic justice.

Information is the greatest weapon in your arsenal to achieve your own economic independence. Supreme Court Justice Learned Hand said, "There are two tax codes in this country. One for those who know it, and one for those who don't."

This same logic holds true for your entire financial security. You have two potential futures in store for you. One, if you plan. And another, if you don't.

I invite you to take this journey into your future with me. I know you're afraid. What you may not know is that we all are.

I have put all of my love for Beth into this project. Her enduring spirit has guided me through the late nights away from my children and the fear that I couldn't do it.

I hope this book gives you some of that strength to conquer your fears as you delight in planning your wonderfully secure retirement.

Acknowledgments

Everything I know, I know because my clients have shared their hopes and dreams, fears and panics with me. All my "book learning" would not be relevant without a purpose in their lives. I want to thank the hundreds of women who have told me their stories and trusted me to help them through their challenges. They are the real storytellers of this book.

As I was being given the opportunity to tell their stories and help thousands more, everyone (and I mean everyone) in my life circled the wagons and encouraged me to do it. At home, my husband, Paul, took over every previously defined "Mom thing." My kids, Lydia and Will, missed Mom a lot but asked with enthusiasm every time they saw me, "How many chapters, Mom?" Their love kept me going.

At the office, Jayshree Patel, Megan White, and Preston Powell watched the shop and kept my door closed so I could work without interruption and have a business to come back to. All my Brownies and their moms let me slide on my leader duties, during cookie season, no less. The rest of my family understood why they didn't see me for a while. What a team!

As I searched for up-to-the-minute facts and data, several people were instantly willing to help: Hope Hagans, Lisa Durham, and Debbie Ayers from the Central Ohio Area Agency on Aging; Wendy Fish and the UU Seniors; Jonathan Fox and Sherman Hanna from Ohio State University; Don Shkolnik, Jill Gianola, Teri Alexander, and Wesley Walker from the Columbus Financial Planning Association; and several sales professionals, whose compliance departments require that they remain anonymous. They know who they are. Thank you!

I can't forget my Sidebar Squad, who scoured the earth for fun and informative facts to include in the book: Julie Dowrey, Ruth Milligan, and Becky Hilbert. Great job!

I'd like to thank the whole editorial team at Pearson, Marie Butler-Knight, Phil Kitchel, Jennifer Chisholm, Mike Sanders, Tom Stevens, Katherin Bidwell, and Cari Luna, for staying with the project and giving me the best experience a new author could have imagined.

Special thanks go to Paula Carlson and Angie Hollerich. Paula typed with excitement for many hours when the deadline loomed. Angie passed me this project and then picked up all the work I didn't have time to do. They were both there every time I asked for help.

I could write another book just about Joe Roberts, who went from project manager to coach to friend. His daily encouragement and guidance made this book a reality. About halfway through he told me, "Edie, this book is going to change lives." It's already changed mine. Thank you, Joe.

Trademarks

All terms mentioned in this book that are known to be or are suspected of being trademarks or service marks have been appropriately capitalized. Alpha Books and Pearson Education, Inc., cannot attest to the accuracy of this information. Use of a term in this book should not be regarded as affecting the validity of any trademark or service mark.

Part 1

Planning for Retirement

So much of our retirement is a mystery. The following questions are probably flying through your thoughts:

- ❖ How soon will I be able to retire?
- ❖ How long will I need to support myself during retirement?
- ❖ Will I be alone?
- ❖ How much will everything cost me then?
- ❖ How do I know how my investments will do between now and then?
- ❖ How can I ever plan when I don't know the answers to these questions?

The answer is that you can plan—and very well. We'll begin slowly and learn some ways to solve this mystery.

Teri and I worked together at what could only be called a cheap motel. It was the job that paid my rent while I started my business. She had burned out on hairstyling and wanted to go into office work. She worked second shift. I worked third.

I would arrive early and she would stay late. We enjoyed talking about the boss and other irritating things. She never made any mistakes, so my job as night auditor was a piece of cake. Balance out, take a nap.

Ten years later my business was going strong. Teri had finally finished her courses in office work. She was having trouble making enough money to really make the break from hairstyling. She had seen me on a local television news show and was calling to see if I needed any help.

Are you kidding? I had struggled constantly with how to find and hire affordable, reliable people. Teri was as predictable as death and taxes.

Before Teri, most of my employees had been students and part-timers. They were bright, energetic, and flexible. But most importantly, they worked for cheap and didn't ask for benefits.

Within a couple of months, Teri had settled into her duties, made friends with the clients, and been hit on a few times by the guys at the bank. Business as usual.

One morning Teri asked to talk with me. I knew this tone of voice. She was going to tell me she was quitting. I hated that. I was going to have to do her work for weeks, while I begged someone else to work for me.

But, it was much worse than that. "How soon are we going to get a 401(k) plan?" she asked. The honeymoon was over. I had survived ten years in business without having to deal with that administrative headache.

"Well," I said, "it is something we need to do. I'm not sure how soon we can afford it. What if I help you set up an IRA in the meantime?"

"It's kind of important," she replied. "Tim came home last night late for dinner. He told me he'd been to see his financial planner. He said he's going to retire at age 55 with a half a million dollars, and if I'm figuring on retiring with him, I had better get started."

Chapter 1

You Are the Planner

This is one job you can't delegate. Your retirement plan is your opportunity to fulfill your own vision of what you want your retirement to look like. No one else has that vision. I will help you clarify and realize that vision.

Whose Job Is It?

It took me a long time to realize what a favor Tim had done for Teri. My initial reaction was outrage. How could a guy be so cruel? This wasn't a marriage! They were roommates having sex, with a piece of paper that said they were allowed to.

But, through his insensitive, immature, controlling, actions, Tim was teaching Teri a very valuable lesson. Her retirement was hers to plan. And she immediately tried to pass the buck to her employer, me.

I caught the pass with a great deal of apprehension. I hadn't even begun to think about my own retirement plan. I had just had my second baby and was still finding my way, building a business as a working mother. Retirement was about as far away as the war that had just started in the Gulf.

Your Employer Is Not Your Planner

I spend my days as a financial counselor helping others forge through the financial and emotional challenges that are keeping them from reaching a sense of financial calm. Retirement is always there as the ultimate goal, but whenever I bring it up, I see looks of disbelief. How can anyone even begin to think about retirement with all the pressures of day-to-day life? And why should they?

As I quiz a client about her retirement plan, 99.9 percent of the time the answer is an explanation of her employer's retirement benefit. Often, it isn't even an accurate understanding. The recurring theme is that it is someone else's job to think about this issue for her.

I rarely get the sense that my client feels at all in control of the process. This feeling is not limited to retirement benefits, but other benefits as well. If her employer doesn't see fit to buy it for her, she must not need it.

Many companies attract workers with the mystique of "great benefits." But workers don't often think beyond whether or not their doctor is on the list of preferred providers. Often on the list of these "great benefits" will be some sort of retirement plan, and that's about all they know.

The Adventure Begins

If you count yourself in the minority of women who have taken the time to ask questions and actually understand what your plan will do, I applaud you. If you have taken it to the next step and figured out what it won't do for you, I am really impressed. If you haven't, be assured that you are very normal and your adventure through retirement planning is just beginning.

It is an exciting adventure, with twists and turns and challenges and risks that will empower you, relax you, and bring a sense of control to your life that you have never experienced before. I don't have to tell you about women who didn't take this journey and who are no longer working. You feel their stress, and maybe you are picking up the pieces for someone who forgot to plan.

We all know what that looks like, and we know we don't want that for our futures. So leave the bag-lady fears at the curb next time you take out the trash. We are going to focus on the excitement and accomplishment of retirement. By the end of this book, you will have made some hard decisions, used a calculator in ways you never dreamed (I won't tell), and put some strategies in place that you will look back on someday and be extremely proud of.

Counselors vs. Planners

It might be helpful to you if you understand a little more about what I've been doing for the last twenty years. I began with three little letters—CLU. In the trade, we know this is three-fifths of a CLUCK, but the fine folks at the American College probably don't appreciate that much! They say it stands for Chartered Life Underwriter. It means I have been tested on and have experience with life and health insurance, employee benefits, and pensions.

The American College

The American College is the nation's oldest and largest institution for higher learning devoted exclusively to distance education for financial services professionals. The American College offers a Certified Financial Planner Education Program to prepare students for the CFP Certification Exam, the Chartered Life Underwriter (CLU), the Chartered Financial Consultant (ChFC), the Registered Employee Benefits Consultant (REBC), the Registered Health Underwriter (RHU), and the Chartered Leadership Fellow (CLF) professional designations. The College also offers the Master of Science in Financial Services (MSFS) graduate degree, certificate programs, and numerous continuing education courses and seminars for those seeking career growth in life insurance and financial services.

Then I added three more little letters—CFP. When I got my CLU twenty years ago, the only people with the CFP were geeky stockbrokers, but it's gained a little speed since then. The Certified Financial Planner Board of Standards gives this out to folks who pass a ten-hour butt-buster exam on personal financial planning. I remember preferring to be in labor about halfway through it.

Certified Financial Planner

The Certified Financial Planner Board of Standards is a nonprofit professional regulatory organization established to benefit the public by fostering professional standards in personal financial planning. The Board owns the following certification marks: CFP and Certified Financial Planner. Individuals who meet initial and ongoing requirements may use them. You can contact the Board at 1-888-237-6275 or www.CFP.net to find out if your planner is certified or has any disciplinary history. You may also file complaints or request free educational brochures.

And my addiction continued when I added three more letters—AFC. These stand for Accredited Financial Counselor. Only two little tests this time, but I just couldn't stop myself. I understand there may be therapy available for this problem.

The Association for Financial Counseling and Planning Education

The Association for Financial Counseling and Planning Education (AFCPE) is a nonprofit, national, organization of individuals who provide financial counseling and financial education services. They promote personal finance education for consumers and professionals. AFCPE certifies professionals, who may use the following marks: Accredited Financial Counselor (AFC), Accredited Housing Counselor (AHC), and Certified Housing Counselor (CHC). Individuals who pass two self-study courses, and meet ongoing experience, ethical, and continuing education requirements may use the marks. You can contact the organization at 614-485-9650, or sburns@finsolve.com, or www.afcpe.org. Free brochures and a complimentary copy of the newsletter are available.

And what does this all mean for you? Well, it means I took the tests so you don't have to. I have a pretty clear view of the difference between financial planning and financial counseling. That's important because I'm the counselor and you're the planner in this book.

Let me explain. Counselors are, by nature, very lazy. We don't *do* anything. Sure, we listen, we talk, we strategize, but the work is yours to do. Planners, on the other hand, are extremely busy people. They collect data, analyze it, prepare plans, monitor them and adjust them. You just show up at the appointments to listen and decide whether or not you like their plan.

Counselors create independence; planners create dependence. When you finish reading this book, I want you to be the most independent creature you have ever been. I will be your counselor, your coach. You will be your own planner. Even if you choose to hire a planner in the future, it will be much less expensive because you've done most of the real work already.

Where We Go from Here

This is an adventure that will take some time. Don't expect to become a financial guru in two hours. We've got fifteen chapters to cover, each packed with terrific strategies that will keep you thinking and get you going toward a successful retirement. I've divided them into three sections, depending upon your starting point.

You are about to finish the first chapter of the first section. There are five more chapters in this section that you should read. Do them one at a time. Pick a time each week to start the chapter. Read it once all the way through. Then go back through holding a pencil and with your calculator on. I will also give you instructions if you already like or would like to learn to use a computer spreadsheet application, such as Excel, to do your planning.

The second section is for you if you are within ten years of your retirement goal date or if you have already retired. Complete these chapters the same way you completed Section I. If your retirement date is farther out, read them through to gain an understanding of what is ahead in your decision-making.

The third section is for you especially if you are already retired. If you haven't retired yet, you will find them helpful to see what issues lie ahead for consideration. You can go ahead and check off some of the items from your life's master To Do List, but you've got some time.

On the other hand, you have very little time to get started on the next chapter. The longer you wait, the harder it will get. You will have fewer options and have to take more risks to arrive at the same destination. So off we go!

Excel

Excel is a computer spreadsheet program manufactured by Microsoft Corporation. It is the best type of program to do fancy calculations. If you've never used it before, you need to see if you have it on your computer. If you are using a computer with Windows, click the Start button in the bottom left of your screen. Then click Programs. To the right, you will see all the programs available on your computer. Excel has a turquoise X to the left of it. If you don't have it, you can purchase it, use it at your local library, or ask a friend if you can stop by and use it when you're ready to try it out.

The Bottom Line

Are you ready? There is no time like right now to begin building the skills that will help you through this process. I'll stay with you and help you through the tough spots, but in the end, it's your job and you're going to be great at it!

When she thinks about it, Louise will tell you her life has looked nothing like what she planned when she was back in high school. Her stories of the Depression sound pretty familiar to the rest of us. Lots of love, not much money.

She worked hard on her studies. Her father made sure her homework was done right or there were consequences. As she walked across the gymnasium to get her diploma, air raid sirens were sounding in Europe and the boys were leaving to fight for the flag. Including William, but she would wait for him. He'd be back.

She couldn't let him fight this war alone, so she went to work in the local factory making medical supplies. She wrote to him every day and dreamed of him every night.

By the time William came back, she was a supervisor making more in a month than her father had made in a year before the war started. William's family's general store had squeaked through the Depression and he took his place as the store's new manager.

As soon as he had enough money for a ring, they were married. She took her savings account and they put money down on a house. She had three babies, one after another. She helped out with the store on weekends when it was busy and her mother could watch the children.

As her children grew, the business grew, too. They opened two more stores in neighboring towns. She did the hiring and bookkeeping for the new stores. She became the first woman president of her town's chamber of commerce.

She never took a real paycheck. Her husband's pay and his share of the store's profit came into their household. She managed all the money. She didn't need her own W-2.

In the mid-70's a large retail chain opened a store in the county. William's sales suffered immediately. They held on as long as they could. The bank helped out for a while and eventually seized the stores, selling the remaining inventory at auction.

There she was, fifty years old with no earnings history on file at Social Security, no college degree, and a tremendous amount of status to live up to in the community.

They both went to work for other businesses in town and she went to college. By the age of 56, she had her masters in counseling and they moved to the state capital so she could work as a school counselor. She retired six years ago, at 71, and now counsels runaways as a volunteer at a halfway house. She visits her grandchildren on weekends.

Chapter 2

A Life View

The mystery of our mortality keeps us guessing most of our lives about the best way to plan. We will use a system that takes out some of the guesswork in order to learn some planning skills.

Counting Backward

It's been said too many times that the only things certain in life are death and taxes. Aren't we lucky that we get to talk about both of them in this book? Death, it seems, is where we should start.

There is a profound change that happens to a human when a doctor pronounces a finite amount of time left to live. The clients I have worked with during this period of their lives express a wisdom that the rest of us can only witness. But even doctors don't really know. Cancer patients can live much longer than expected. And people who "recover fully" from heart surgery can die the next week in a car wreck.

Would you really want to know how long you have left to live? Some dread the idea that they will outlive their mental or physical functioning. "I hope I don't live that long." Or you might hear someone delight at the idea of living past 100 and having Willard Scott wish them a happy birthday.

Starting at the end and working backward is not a natural way to think about things. We think of the progression of time as moving from birth to death. We report our ages as the number of years since our first breath. We could count down, instead of up, reporting how many years we have left until our last breath. That is, of course, if we knew when our last breath would be.

Getting Gray

You are not the only one who is getting more and more gray. The percentage of the population over 65 has doubled from 6 percent to 12 percent during the time that the Social Security program has been in effect. And the first baby boomers are just now turning 60. Investing in Miss Clairol might not be a bad idea!

Your best clue to your longevity is your family tree. Take a look at how long your parents and grandparents spent in this life. Then add years for your daily exercise, wonderful diet, avoidance of tobacco and alcohol, and great preventive healthcare. Oh! You don't do all those proven life-extenders? Well, your calculator has a subtract button, too.

Our medical researchers have been working hard over the last half-century to find ways to keep us alive longer. It is now estimated that if you can make it until 60 without developing diabetes, heart disease, or cancer, you've got a straight shot at 95! Yes, I know the average life expectancy isn't that high, but the way statistics work, the longer you live, the higher your life expectancy is. Since those three diseases have tons of risk factors that you can control, you do have some say in the matter.

So, your first job in planning your retirement is to pick a number. It should be more than your current age and less than 120, let's say. Pick one that makes you happy. Or pick a year you want to see. Or, an event you hope you live long enough to witness, like your one-year-old granddaughter's graduation from medical school.

There's no jackpot if you get it right. No one is going to show up at your funeral to congratulate you. But your planning process will be very calm. You can pretend you are as wise as those whose end time has been officially documented in a doctor's chart.

On the timeline below I'd like you to mark your current age. Then mark your self-determined life expectancy—your deathdate. Now take the difference between the two. This is the number of years you have left. Divide it by 5: that's how many more cars you'll probably have. By 15: the number of dogs. No one's given me a good average for the number of men.

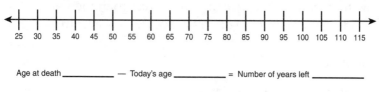

Age at death_____ — Today's age _____ = Number of years left _____

Your planning timeline.

First You Work, Then You Don't

A recent commercial for a high-speed Internet service portrays a young man at his graduation. His proud parents are wondering, "So, have you decided what you are going to do with your life?" "I've been doing some research," he replies, "and this retirement thing looks promising." Skip some steps, the commercial advises.

We smile as we watch this commercial because it's cute. We know a young woman would never be so smug. It's such a guy thing to assume the world owes him a retirement without working for it. Women have always worked hard, and worked hard well past the year their husbands retire. The old saying, "A woman's work is never done," reminds us that there have always been gender differences when it comes to work.

Imagine your grandmother sitting down and planning the year that she would stop cleaning, cooking, gardening, serving her church, or caring for sick relatives. She worked until somebody made her stop. And then she complained.

Many women have retired from their paying careers to begin their careers as mothers. As their nest empties they experience the psychological retirement that men feel as they walk into the social security office. They cure their separation pains with new work to keep them vital.

But you are not your grandmother. You work for money. You don't want to do that work your entire life. You can see a time period when you are not working in your current job, but still active and eager to keep growing, exploring, and living.

And you can also see a time that you won't be so active. You know that women live several years longer than men on the average and spend more time disabled. This means eventually becoming dependent upon family, home health caregivers, or nursing home staff.

High vs. Low Retirement

So all retirement is not created equal. Let's call the first period High Retirement. Like the high life, high hopes and dreams are realized. Following that we have Low Retirement, a period of lower functioning, lower activity, and lower hopes.

The type and amount of financial expenditures in these two retirement periods can be very different. High Retirement can include travel, volunteer work, entertainment, pampering grandkids and new hobbies. Downsizing, medical expenses, and caregiving expenses mark Low Retirement.

Census figures estimate the average number of years that women spend in Low Retirement to be seven. Go back to your timeline and put another mark seven years before your deathdate. This will be important later as we calculate your financial needs during retirement.

Now you should have three marks on your timeline. Let's label them *a* today's age; *d* age of Low Retirement; and *e* age of death. So what happened to *b* and *c* you'd like to know? I've saved the best for last.

Let's work on *c* first. This is the day of your retirement party, the gold watch date. This is the most distinct, determinable date in your planning process. Other than today, which is a given, this is the date you have the most control over. You may have thought of this date as the date you "qualify" for social security (see the following table), the date you get "full benefits" from your pension, or the date your husband has picked to retire.

Age Eligible to Receive Full Social Security Retirement Benefits

Year of Birth	Age
1937 or before	65yrs
1938	65yrs/2mos
1939	65yrs/4mos
1940	65yrs/6mos
1941	65yrs/8mos
1942	65yrs/10mos
1943-1954	66yrs
1955	66yrs/2mos
1956	66yrs/4mos
1957	66yrs/6mos
1958	66yrs/8mos
1959	66yrs/10mos
1960 or after	67yrs

Life Expectancy

When Congress passed the Social Security Act in 1935 the average life expectancy of workers was less than 65. Its intent was to help support people who outlived their working years. As the life expectancy extended, it became a base for our retirement planning. Retirement periods of ten, twenty, or thirty years are very new phenomena that the Social Security Trust fund is struggling to keep up with.

If you were free to ignore the financial considerations, you could walk away from your job almost any time you please. Slavery was outlawed several generations ago. Forced retirement, layoffs, and early buyouts are still common, however. So, you can leave as early as you like, but you may not be able to stay as long as you would like.

Jo Ann Davidson

Ohio's Speaker of the House of Representatives, Jo Ann Davidson, was just forced out of her job by term limits. At 73, she was eager and willing to continue her important work. She is still very electable and employable, but you may not find a waiting market for your skills at that age.

Since you have a reasonable amount of control over this date, it will require a little more thought. Once again, you can count forward or backward. Counting forward would involve deciding how much time you want to spend continuing to work. Counting backward would involve deciding how much time you want to spend in High Retirement.

Only you can balance these two notions. You've heard friends say they want to retire while they can still enjoy their retirement: meaning that they don't want to skip the step of High Retirement and go directly from work into Low Retirement. On the other hand, a High Retirement period of thirty years might seem terribly boring to you. You can find your happy medium.

I need to explain that some people use the word *retirement* in a way that complicates our model. They have a career in which they have worked since school, maybe even for the same employer since graduation. They will qualify for a retirement benefit after thirty years and they plan to quit that job at that time. Then they will go do what they really want to do. People *retire* from the military, school systems, police forces, and large corporations this way. The beginning of their High Retirement, however, is when they quit the next job. If, however, they retire and what they really want to do is better categorized as a hobby making very little money compared to what they earned in their career, their High Retirement has begun.

So, for your timeline, *c* will be the date that you will no longer be taking home a regular paycheck that could support you by itself. Put that on your timeline. Based upon your planning, you may find that you would like to plan to have income from a part-time job to supplement your retirement income. We will count that income as another source of retirement money.

High vs. Low Savings

Let's review.

a = Today

b = ?

c = High Retirement

d = Low Retirement

e = Death

Have I left you in excruciating suspense? What in the world could *b* be? This is the date that financial planners leave out of their careful formulas. They assume that just because you're worried about retirement, that you have any ability to do something about it today. And that it will immediately become the *number one priority* in your life, above car repairs, birth control pills, and visiting grandma on her birthday. Not!

Oh, you can do *something* about it, and you already are by reading this far into this book! But, I bet you are fully expecting that we are going to do a lot of complicated math just to determine that in order to retire, you are going to have to put half your paycheck in your 401(k) plan. At that point your hidden talent, *attitude*, will take over and you will declare that I am nuts and you have to do what you have to do and that's that! Problem solved, back to doing what you've been doing.

Instead, let's find a new way to think about retirement planning. It's totally acceptable to have as part of your plan a period of time that you are not saving enough to fully reach your goals. We will call this your Low Savings period. You may take other steps in your plan during this time to secure your retirement, like getting your kids out of the house and on their own so you aren't supporting their kids in your retirement. You might be paying off your mortgage and retiring that annoying credit card debt. You might be finishing your degree so that your income will be significantly increased for the rest of your earning years. You might even be paying off the attorney that got you out from under an abusive marriage that drained your ability to focus on your future at all.

You've heard all the hype about saving early and how you have to save a gazillion more dollars each month if you start later. It's true, but what it doesn't address is you and your previous decisions that you can't change. So don't beat yourself up if you've got some stuff to take care of first. What happened is what happened. Period.

Effect of Early Saving

To save a half-million dollars by age 70, a worker would have to start saving $90/week at age 20, $125/week at age 30, $200/week at age 40. You get the point. Keep reading and you'll learn how to figure this out for yourself.

Take a quick inventory of your stuff: the debt, the kids, the education, and anything that you would use to end this statement, "I can't save for retirement because _____." Use the following table. That's your stuff. And you have to deal with it.

I Can't Save for Retirement Because ....

Stuff	Years to Take Care of

Then flip the statement, "When I take care of ___(my stuff)___, I'll be able to save for retirement." It's much more fun to talk in the positive. This brings us to the mysterious letter *b*. How long will it reasonably take you to take care of your stuff? Two years to finish your degree? Three years to pay off the credit cards? Six years until the kids are gone? Give yourself another year to relax and then go for it! Mark that date on your timeline. This is the beginning of your High Savings period.

Notice that the two periods are called Low Savings and High Savings; not No Savings and Mega Savings. You are going to start saving, if you haven't already. It's sort of like swimming in the shallow end. You'll get to know what the water feels like and begin to develop your comfort in it. And you'll see how much fun the folks are having going off the high dive. You'll want to do it too, even though it looks scary.

So, we've divided your life into five chunks. The first is the time that has already passed. It's history, done, over. You're not going to change it, but you may have lingering stuff to fix. You're going to fix it during your Low Savings period. Then you will enter your High Savings period, working hard and keeping focused on your goals. Then comes High Retirement with all its rewards and excitement. Then, you will fully ripen during your Low Retirement, slowing down as you approach your deathdate.

Is your life going to follow the exact dates you are picking for this planning process. No, not likely, but it doesn't matter. What you are learning is a process with lots of variables that we don't know exactly. It's an adventure, remember? We don't really know what is going to happen. We want to be able to take advantage of new opportunities along the way. The only way for that to happen is to have a basic plan to work from. So we have to pretend some of the unknowns are known in order to make it workable.

Now, using the following table, let's calculate how many years are in each period:

Low Savings period	_____ yrs.	$b - a$
High Savings period	_____ yrs.	$c - b$
High Retirement period	_____ yrs.	$d - c$
Low Retirement period	_____ yrs.	$e - d$

Will Your Money Work for You?

For the first two periods, you are working for your money. In the last two periods, your money is working for you.

You get up each morning and go to work. In exchange for spending energy on an activity that someone else values, you get money. You could be paid with other forms of compensation. People in the military get housing, food, clothing, medical services and free travel. You could also receive the "benefit" of group purchases your employer makes on your behalf, such as daycare services, dental care and a parking space.

Then you can choose to trade your money for goods and services from other people. But if you choose to spend less than you earn, you can send the money left over to work for you. It's a very simple concept. When you accumulate enough of it, it gets up in the morning and goes to work so you don't have to.

Money that you accumulate for this purpose is called capital. Capital is money that you never intend to spend. Because, if you spend it, it can't go to work for you anymore. Up until a couple of years ago, most of the capital accumulated on behalf of workers in this country was under somebody else's control. Pension funds, government funds or insurance companies had our money and told us when and how much we got of it.

But, now, much of the money is back in our control. Not only can we get to our retirement money, but we have to make the withdrawal and investment decisions. This leaves us open to two risks not there before. The first is that we will steal it for other reasons. The second is that we will not manage it with the diligence that the paid managers provided in earlier decades.

It's kind of like being our own bosses. We have to tell ourselves to get out of bed and get to work. We have to tell ourselves what our job is and determine when we've done it well. If you've ever tried working for yourself, you know what a lousy boss you are. This is a problem.

Ask yourself, "If I were my money, would I work for me?" Are you clear in your expectations? Do you have regular supervisory meetings where you allow it to vent its frustrations? Do you throw nice holiday parties?

By the end of this book, you are going to be a great boss! Your money will work wonderfully for you. You will look back with pride on the years you spent earning it and delight in the retirement you have designed for yourself.

The Bottom Line

Even though you still don't know exactly when you will enter the next three periods of your retirement plan, you can begin to see a plan emerging. Confronting the reality of your own mortality and morbidity is truly the hardest part of this process. Congratulations and on to the numbers!

When Patricia's kids aren't asking her for money, the electric company is. She feels on top of things when she remembers what day it is, let alone knows what her balance is in her checking account.

Patricia has raised two teenagers, pretty much by herself. Her ex-husband steps in and out of their lives at his convenience. Patricia is still paying the attorney fees for the last round in court over unpaid child support.

Patricia works for a great company as a quality control specialist. She knows if she lost this job, she wouldn't have much luck finding the same income in today's job market.

Every year the benefits department sends around that pretty brochure explaining all the nice things they're doing for her. All those little boxes are so hard to figure out, but she knows she should be checking more of them. When she thinks about her net paycheck she wonders how she could do without any more of it. She already pays for her kids' health insurance since her ex-husband never keeps a job long enough to qualify.

Last year she decided to join the 401(k) plan and she checked the 2 percent box that let her receive a match from her company. She knows she's worked this long and has only accumulated $2,000 in her retirement fund. She doesn't want her ex-husband to know, for fear he'll use it against her in court.

The kids are going to be ready for college soon and both of them seem eager to attend. She seems to get her bills paid, pretty much on time, but isn't proud of her credit report.

She knows she only has another ten or fifteen years before she can retire on her company's pension. But she knows that it will only be about a third of her current income. She's not sure how much social security will pay her. Her 401(k) plan won't have enough by then to really make much of a difference.

Sometimes she thinks about getting a part-time job, but then she wonders what trouble the girls would get into while she's away. She wishes her ex-husband would step up to the plate and do his part. She knows she'll be on her own someday with very little security.

She worries about being dependent upon her children at a time in their lives when they're caring for their children. She wants to be a fun grandma, but she won't be able to take the kids to Disney World. It's hard to say no to her daughters now and she wonders how she'll say no to her grandkids then.

Chapter 3

A Balancing Act

Numbers can be nasty and budgets can be boring. Not this time! Grabbing all the numbers is essential to filling in the details of your retirement vision. We break up your budget into easy-to-think-about pieces that will help you build your plan.

Your Lifestyle Now

Gathering Numbers

I have spent over 20,000 hours asking people number questions, and not getting number answers. It takes me a while to catch on to things. I wrote Bill Gates and asked him if the next generation of computers could have, instead of the numbers, keys that say:

❖ Way too much!

❖ More than I should.

❖ Not as much as he does.

❖ Heck if I know!

❖ Yeah, right.

❖ I had that here somewhere.

❖ I don't want to know.

❖ Yeah, I guess I do spend money on that.

❖ Are you kidding?

❖ That's a sore subject.

As interesting as the emotions behind the numbers are, they really don't compute as well as good old-fashioned numbers. You know, the kind they teach on Sesame Street—brought to you today by the number seven.

Now I know that one of you reading this book has a nice Quicken report sitting in front of you that goes back to the beginning of time, or at least the beginning of Quicken. Congratulations, you win the jackpot and get to skip a couple of pages. So, go get a cup of tea, while the rest of us catch up with you.

Okay. For the rest of you who wouldn't know a Quicken report any more than you would recognize your county coroner, we've got some calculating to do. Remember my instructions in Chapter 1: read through the chapter first, and then come back and fill in the charts.

The goal of this exercise is to begin to balance your current lifestyle with your retirement lifestyle. Most people get really used to themselves by the time they retire. Some people call this being set in their ways. Well, have you ever noticed somebody who is set in her ways really enjoying change? Try switching their silverware in the drawer sometime. Put the knives on the right and the forks on the left. Then go see a movie, because you don't want to be around the next time that they set the table.

Well, guess what? Odds are, you'll be just like that by the time you retire, if you aren't already. So, what this means is that you don't want to take a big jump up or down when you retire. You'll want things to be just about the same. You might move to a nicer climate, but you'll still arrange your silverware the same way. I'm going to teach you how to find that balance, but I have to ask you some number questions and you have to answer in numbers, because Mr. Gates threw away my letter.

Your lifestyle includes so many intangible things: your religious beliefs, your relationships, your passions, and your fears, for starters. Your underlying financial stability gives you the freedom to live life true to what gives it meaning for you. Money is a means to an end, not an end in itself. Don't lose sight of that or think for one minute that I don't believe it.

Your Income

As much as you'd like to write down your last direct deposit on the following chart, it won't do. We're going to need to get out the pay stub and look at that big number that you never get to touch, your gross pay. Another way to do this is to look at your W-2 earnings. We want to end up with a monthly average for our analysis. So multiply the gross earnings on one stub by the number of paydays each year and then divide by twelve—or take the W-2 earnings and divide by twelve.

Include all your current sources of income. You will need to decide if you are including your partner's income in this analysis. It may be helpful to do it both ways. You will want to plan for a joint retirement, but you should be comfortable knowing that if the relationship doesn't make it to retirement, that you will be fine.

Income Calculations

Sources of Income	Yearly Amount/12	= Monthly Amount
_____	_____	_____
_____	_____	_____
_____	_____	_____
_____	_____	_____
_____	_____	_____
_____	_____	_____

continues

Income Calculations (continued)

Sources of Income	Yearly Amount/12	= Monthly Amount
_____	_____	_____
_____	_____	_____
Total Monthly Income		_____

Your Payroll Deductions

Since you already have your pay stubs out, this should be fairly simple. Write down each item you pay for through your payroll department on the chart below. To calculate the monthly costs, multiply each item by how many times a year it comes out and divide by twelve. Since this is a retirement planning process, leave the retirement fund deposit off of this chart. It will get its own special spot later. Total all the monthly items to get your monthly payroll deductions.

Payroll Deduction Calculations

Payroll Deductions	Yearly Amount/12	= Monthly Amount
_____	_____	_____
_____	_____	_____
_____	_____	_____
_____	_____	_____
_____	_____	_____
_____	_____	_____
_____	_____	_____
Total Monthly Deductions		_____

Your Frequent Expenses

This is the stuff that kills you. Grab a twenty from the magic money machine and six hours later, you'll be damned if you can remember where it went. I can't imagine any more horrifying torture than having to figure out where it goes. You've tried all the systems out there—only write checks, write down everything you spend, only use a debit or credit card so you have bill to track it, use envelopes with cash—and you still don't have a clue!

So here's what we do. You pick a day. Next payday makes sense to me. Go to the bank and get out a round number, like $100, $200, or $250. Then spend it. Are you with me so far?

Only spend it on things that you do on a regular basis. Food, parking, videos, school lunches, gasoline, eating out, and so on. *Do not* use your credit or debit card or checks for these things until the cash is gone. And don't buy anything unusual with the money, like a wedding present or beer for the Super Bowl party.

Then come back and tell me how many days it lasted. When it's gone, take out the same amount and do it again. In research they call this replicating your findings. Did it last the same number of days? If not, which was more accurate? Try it again if you like. When you get a number you like, do this: Divide the amount you took out by the number of days it lasted and multiply by 30. This is the monthly amount for your frequent expenses. See the following chart.

Frequent Expenses Calculation

Amount of cash you took out of the bank	_____
Divided by:	
Number of days your cash lasted	_____
Average cash spent per day =	_____
Multiply by 30:	
Monthly frequent expenditures =	_____

Your Periodic Expenses

Well, this one's a little harder. You will have to do some thinking or dreaming about this category. These are the nonbill items in your life. They might come on a credit card statement, but they are infrequent and unpredictable. The following chart has some very common categories that make sense to most women. If they don't make sense to you, change them, add some, or start over with your own list. Some of my clients call this the stuff that "comes up" when you least want it to.

History is great, if you've got it, but only to help us predict the future. Your imagination works fine, too. Close your eyes and think about the next year of your life. How much will you be spending on medical expenses? What do you want to spend on clothes? What is your vacation going to cost? Don't deny that your car will need to be maintained and that your house breaks, too. Be very honest. This is important.

Most of these expenses don't happen often enough to think about them monthly, so write down a yearly number that makes you comfortable (see the following chart). Then divide them by twelve. Add them up and you have your monthly periodic expense number.

Periodic Expenses Calculation

Periodic Expenses	Yearly Amount/12	= Monthly Amount
Medical/dental	_____	_____
Car repairs	_____	_____
Home repairs	_____	_____
Clothing	_____	_____
Gifts	_____	_____
Hobbies	_____	_____
Vacations	_____	_____
_____	_____	_____
Monthly Periodic Expenses:		_____

Your Bills

This category is for things that you pay very regularly, that usually come in the mail. Let's leave out payments on debt, however.

I want to treat them separately because they will end before retirement, hopefully. This category is for things that you will *want* to have forever. Two exceptions are the mortgage payment and car payment. Put them here because housing and transportation expenses may continue even after you retire the initial debt.

Again, I have given you a list of common categories. Make it your own. Many bills are paid monthly, but some aren't. And some monthly bills vary in their amounts. Your assignment is to come up with an average monthly amount, for the future. If you have just replaced your old inefficient furnace, don't use last year's heating bills as an average. Once you are happy with each item, add up the averages. This is your monthly bill expense.

Bill Expense Calculation

Bill Expense	Quarterly Amount/3 = Monthly Amount	
Mortgage/Rent	_____	_____
Car loan/Lease	_____	_____
Church contribution	_____	_____
Daycare/Tuition	_____	_____
Electricity	_____	_____
Heating expense	_____	_____
Telephone	_____	_____
Cable/Internet	_____	_____
Life insurance	_____	_____
Car insurance	_____	_____
_____	_____	_____
_____	_____	_____
_____	_____	_____
Monthly Bill Expenses:		_____

Your Debts

If you haven't got any, move to the next section. Oh, you're still here. Thanks for staying to keep me company. You've seen those amazing disappearing acts that those cute magicians pull off. Well, we're going to make your debt disappear! Let's find out when it will be gone:

❖ Find the latest statements from your credit cards, installment loans, student loans, and other debt.

❖ Don't forget to include any old bills you owe and personal/family loans you need to repay someday.

❖ List them all on the following chart.

❖ Put their balance/payoff/principal in the next column.

❖ Put their interest rate (e.g. .08, .169) in column 3.

❖ Multiply Column 2 by Column 3 and divide by 12 to get the monthly interest they are charging you. Put it in column 4.

❖ List the minimum payment they expect each month in column 5 (even if you like to pay more.)

❖ Total columns 2, 4, and 5.

Debt Calculation

Column 1	Column 2	Column 3	Column 4	Column 5
Creditor	Total Owed	Interest Rate	Monthly Interest	Minimum Payment
_____	_____ ×	_____ /12 =	_____	_____
_____	_____ ×	_____ /12 =	_____	_____
_____	_____ ×	_____ /12 =	_____	_____
_____	_____ ×	_____ /12 =	_____	_____
_____	_____ ×	_____ /12 =	_____	_____
_____	_____ ×	_____ /12 =	_____	_____
_____	_____ ×	_____ /12 =	_____	_____
_____	_____ ×	_____ /12 =	_____	_____
_____	_____ ×	_____ /12 =	_____	_____
_____	_____ ×	_____ /12 =	_____	_____
Totals	_____(C)	_____	_____(A)	_____(B)

We now know three things:

❖ The total amount of debt you have (C).

❖ The total amount of interest you are being charged each month (A).

❖ The total minimum amount you can pay each month (B).

We can do a lot with this information to help you plan your retirement. First, let's find out how long it will take you to retire the debt using the minimum they are asking for. If you continue to pay that amount (even though they may ask for less in the future) and your interest rates stay about the same, this formula will give you a good approximation of when you will be out of debt. Using the following chart, fill in A, B, and C with the amounts in A, B, and C of the preceding chart.

Out-of-Debt Date Calculation

(A) _____ × .60 =	(D) _____	
(B) _____ −	(D) _____ =	(E) _____
(C) _____ /	(E) _____ =	
Number of months left to be in debt.		_____

Did that shock you? Did you think it would be a lot longer? Maybe you want to go back to Chapter 2, "A Life View," and change the date for your High Savings period. You may be out of debt before you thought. This assumes that you pay that same amount every month for that many months. *And* you finance future expenses from your periodic expenses budget instead of using credit. This takes a disciplined savings habit, but that's what we're learning all the way through this book.

Maybe that date is farther in the future than you would like? Let's do the calculation again and this time add $50 to the monthly payment (use A, B, and C from the preceding chart for A, B, and C in the following chart to find D and E). What does that do to your time left to be in debt?

Out-of-Debt Date Recalculation

(A) _____ × .60 =   (D) _____

(B) _____ −   (D) _____ =   (E) _____

(C) _____ /   (E) _____ + $50 =   _____

New number of months left to be in debt.   _____

Or

(C) _____ /   (E) _____ + $100 =   _____

New number of months left to be in debt.   _____

You may want to think about this for a couple of days before we move on. When do you want to be out of debt? Play with the formula a little. What happens if you add $100 instead of $50. Are there $100 of expenses you can cut for that many months and get this part of your financial life behind you? As soon as it is over, the entire monthly payment will be free to help you reach your retirement goals. It's worth some thought.

Add It All Up

Copy the totals from the six expense summary charts into the first column of the next chart. And here is the special place for your retirement savings number. Write in the actual amount you are currently saving.

Expense Summary

Category	Low Savings	High Savings	High Retirement	Low Retirement
Total income	_____	_____	_____	_____
Payroll deductions	_____	_____	_____	_____
Frequent expenses	_____	_____	_____	_____
Periodic expenses	_____	_____	_____	_____

Expense Summary

Category	Low Savings	High Savings	High Retirement	Low Retirement
Bill expenses	_____	_____	_____	_____
Debt payments	_____	_____	_____	_____
Retirement savings	_____	_____	_____	_____
Amount left over	_____	_____	_____	_____

Subtract all the expenses from your income and see if you are short or over. If you are short, you have three choices:

❖ Increase your income

❖ Decrease your expenses or payment on debt

❖ Go into more debt

As much as this hurts to think about, it is better to get a handle on it now, than just continue to incur debt until retirement. With your new focus on your future financial security, you may find some deeper motivation to make some tough choices.

If you have extra, you have just found some additional money to put away for retirement. But it may not feel like it. Work with the numbers for a couple of months before you increase your savings. The worst decision would be to save too much for retirement and then have to borrow it back out because you haven't managed your current expenses well. This costs you in ways you couldn't imagine.

Your Lifestyle Then

Time to get out your crystal ball. See if you can find it. The last time I saw mine, a kid was using it for Nerf gun target practice. Dust it off and wind it up.

Look at the other three columns on the last chart. Go back to where you calculated each of the income and expense items. What will be different in each of the next three periods: High Savings, High Retirement, and Low Retirement?

Wait, we have to have a heart-to-heart talk about inflation. This is one of those facts of life like the school nurse told you about in fourth grade. And just like those facts, it is a little different than what you think. Or what your friends have told you.

Inflation is *not* a rise in the price of things. It is one *reason* that prices may go up, but not the only one. Inflation is what we call the situation when your money is worth less. This can happen for a lot of reasons, which are too complicated for me to explain. I didn't really go to my economics classes; I just graduated in it. There's a difference.

I can give you an example, however. In the last few years, inflation has been very low, around 3 percent. But the price of college tuition around the country has increased at a rate of 7 percent. So the first 3 percent of the increase is due to inflation, but the other 4 percent is due to something else. It could be that the research grants are less, so the students have to pay more, or any number of reasons.

So, in a year that inflation is 3 percent, if you get a 3 percent raise, you didn't get a raise. Your money was worth 3 percent less, so your employer raised the amount back up to what you were earning before. You should notice that the new amount is buying the same amount of stuff you bought last year with the lower amount.

And in the same year, if your savings account is earning 3 percent interest, you have exactly the same amount of money at the end of the year as you did at the beginning. Get it?

So, I'm going to make this real simple. Forget it. Don't think about inflation when you look into your crystal ball. Yeah, I know hamburgers are going to cost $42.50 when you retire. I don't care. Not for this exercise. If we can't get the numbers figured out in "today's dollars" we don't have a chance at doing it with inflation figured in.

Just like the nurse said, "When you get a little older, you'll understand."

Back to the chart. Turn up the power on the crystal ball. See yourself in each period. How much are you making? Who are you feeding? Where are you traveling? What makes you happy? How much does it cost? Where are you living? If it helps you to write, you could write a short story about yourself in each period. Then do that person's expense charts.

You may have to do some additional research to find out the income numbers after retirement. The Social Security Administration, Public Pension Funds and your employer's pension administrator can give you estimated numbers for your income at retirement. Most of these calculations will give you amounts in today's dollars, just as you are projecting your expenses. This works out well for our purposes. When your actual retirement date arrives, your benefits will have been adjusted for inflation along the way.

Social Security Statement

Each year you are supposed to receive a statement from the Social Security Administration that projects your retirement income. This is a relatively new practice, ordered by Congress. You won't get one if you are being audited or the IRS has a wrong address for you. And the one you get will assume certain income from now until a standard retirement date. It's a really good idea to order one that is more accurate, with *your* desired retirement date and *your* projection of earnings. Call 1-800-772-1213 or www.SSA.gov.

About this point in the planning process, you will feel like asking if there are average percentages that we can use to increase or decrease expenses in each period. Yep, there are. But you aren't average, so you don't get to use them. Sorry, nice try, but I refuse to help you strive to be average. You need to be you and stay that way.

Calculating the Difference

Your goal is to end up with a zero at the bottom of each of the columns after you subtract the expenses from the income. This means that when your earned income stops, you will be taking money from your retirement funds to balance out. It looks like this:

Expense Summary Sample

Category	Low Savings	High Savings	High Retirement	Low Retirement
Total income	$3,050	$3,300	$1,980	$1,980
Less:				
Payroll deductions	$650	$700	$50	$50
Frequent expenses	$650	$650	$650	$450
Periodic expenses	$250	$350	$550	$300
Bill expenses	$1100	$1100	$1100	$3000
Debt payments	$350	--	--	--
Leaves:				
Retirement savings	$50	$500	-$370	-$1820
	Per month for 5 years	Per month for 14 years	Per month for 18 years	Per month for 7 years

The four numbers we will work with in future chapters are the ones next to retirement savings on your chart. The first two should be positive, meaning you are adding to your capital. The second two will probably be negative, meaning that you are letting your capital support you.

You've done a lot of work. Let's copy your retirement savings numbers into the following chart and bring forward the numbers from Chapter 2 that tell us how many years you will have for each period.

Expense Summary Completed

Category	Low Savings	High Savings	High Retirement	Low Retirement
Total income	_____	_____	_____	_____
Less				
Payroll deductions	_____	_____	_____	_____
Frequent expenses	_____	_____	_____	_____
Periodic expenses	_____	_____	_____	_____
Bill expenses	_____	_____	_____	_____
Debt payments	_____	_____	_____	_____
Leaves				
Retirement savings	_____	_____	_____	_____
	Per month for	Per month for	Per month for	Per month for
Number of years	_____	_____	_____	_____

Excel Instructions for Chart

Open up a new worksheet. Click File, Save As. Type RetPlan. Click Save. Save the worksheet periodically as you work with your numbers. That will keep your work for later.

Copy the column and row names from my chart above. You can make columns wider by positioning your mouse on the line in-between the letters at the top of the column. You will see a crossed arrow. Click and drag to the right.

You can let the spreadsheet add up your numbers for you by doing the following:

1. Write down the address (letter of column and number of row) of the cells that hold the following information:

    Low Savings: Total Income _____ [A]

    Low Savings: Payroll Deductions _____ [B]

    Low Savings: Debt Payments _____ [C]

2. Put your mouse in the Low Savings Retirement cell and click.

3. Type the following formula, substituting the cell addresses you wrote down above for A, B, and C

    +[A]–@SUM([B].[C]), then hit Enter.

4. Click the Copy icon (two sheets of paper) at the top. Move your mouse to the High Savings Retirement cell and click. Click the Paste icon (a clipboard with a piece of paper).

5. Repeat step 4 for the High Retirement and Low Retirement cells.

You may be coming back to this chapter as we learn more about each decision that will affect your expenses. For example, you may decide to purchase long-term care insurance that will increase your expenses now, but decrease your expenses in Low Retirement. You may change the taxability of some of your investments that will reduce your tax expense in payroll deductions. This is a work in progress.

The numbers you have calculated will help you continue to learn how to plan, but you may decide that you want to change them as we get farther into this. Remember, what you are learning is a process, not an event. My hope is that you can revisit this process throughout your retirement planning period whenever you have important decisions to make.

The Bottom Line

Now don't tell me that was more information than you wanted to know! Whether the numbers scared you or surprised you, you have a big jump on bringing them into control. You will revise these charts many times as you make informed, proactive decisions.

For her eighth birthday, Sharon's grandparents gave her a ten-dollar bill and a shiny new silver dollar. The next day her mother took her to the bank to deposit her money from Grandma and Grandpa. She had her own little book in a little case that she'd had for a long time. She thinks they gave it to her when she was born. Her mom said she was old enough to walk up to the counter and make the deposit by herself. Mrs. Dunham had worked at the bank for as long as Sharon could remember and always knew what flavor lollipop Sharon liked so she went to her line.

She waited for the person in front of her to be done and then she handed Mrs. Dunham her new ten-dollar bill and said, "Can you put this in my bank, please?" As she stood there, she remembered the dollar coin and thought, "Well I'll probably just lose it so I'll give it to Mrs. Dunham to keep, too." So she said, "Wait a minute. Can you keep this, too?" Mrs. Dunham said, "Sure," and gave her back her book with $11 written in it. It also had another $.60 that Mrs. Dunham said was interesting or something like that. Sharon knew that sometimes the bank made deposits for her because she was a good customer. She went home, put her book back in her dresser drawer, and ran down the street to play with her friends.

She thought about her coin sometimes. She knew it was safe in that big room in the back of the bank. The one with the big door with a steering wheel on it. She knew they closed that door every night to keep the robbers out. In the morning, when Mrs. Dunham and the rest of the people got to the bank, they opened it up and everything was safe.

One day, she was at the bank with her mom and she thought, "I'd like to see my dollar coin." So she went up and asked Mrs. Dunham if she could go get it for her. Mrs. Dunham said, "Oh honey, we don't have your dollar coin. We don't keep the money in our bank. We send it to another bank, a bigger bank." "Well, when can I get it back?" she said. Mrs. Dunham explained that she could give her a different dollar coin but it wouldn't be the one that she brought in that day. "But, my grandma gave it to me. It's mine. I'm never giving you any money ever again!"

Chapter 4

Trust

Learning to plan for retirement is learning to trust. Who to trust and how much to trust them are hard questions. The more you understand about how your banks, investments and governments work, the easier it will become to know the answers.

It's What Makes Us Unique

So, how old were you when you figured out that the bank didn't just put your money in the big room in the back and give it back to you when you wanted it? That's a pretty startling revelation for most of us. And what on earth could they be doing with your money when they send it to that bigger bank?

Remember the bank of your childhood? It probably had that yellow sign telling everyone it was a fallout shelter. They were huge, strong, buildings that gave us a sense that our money was safe inside those walls. I didn't really know what *fallout* was, but I was sure that if the bank could protect me from it, they could sure keep my money there.

When I think about all the things that set humans apart from other species on this planet, trust makes it to the top of my list.

Imagine this: You hand your dog a treat and explain to him that he should bank this treat for a later date. So you send him next door to give it to the neighbor dog. And try to convince him that the neighbor dog will hold onto it for him. It's such an absurd notion when we apply it to any critters but ourselves.

But we do learn to trust each other. We build buildings, create slogans, hire actors, and public relations firms to make each other believe that we are to be trusted. Then we spend a lot of money through our taxes hiring regulators to make sure we can be trusted and we tell our lawmakers to establish and protect our currency that we all respect.

Trusting Advisors

Almost half of women surveyed said they worried about trusting their financial advisors.

—Ernst & Young's Financial Planning for Women

The Alternative Doesn't Sound Fun

Squirrels don't retire. There isn't a moment in their short lives when they can afford to stop doing what they do, gathering food. They have, however, figured out how to hide their food so that other squirrels won't eat it. Squirrels don't usually join together to create a common bank of nuts that they'll all share in later. They have their own stash, they know where it is, and they trust no one with it. They may have some easier places to hide their food, but by their very nature those places that are easy are also risky.

For our economy to work—and by the way for your retirement to work, too—we have to learn to trust. First, we learn that a green picture of a dead president peeking through that little envelope means money and that someone else will give us something for that money. Next, we learn that there are different presidents on different pieces of paper and that they mean different things. Eventually, we move on to learning that numbers in a bankbook or on a bank statement mean the same thing. And now, we've had to learn that electronic signals turning on a light on a video display terminal mean the same thing.

The Federal Reserve System

A very small portion of our supply of money is actually in green pictures of dead presidents. Most of it is in electronic deposits at the banks of the Federal Reserve System. Somebody probably told you at some point in your life that money doesn't grow on trees, but it does grow at the Federal Reserve.

There are some things about the Federal Reserve that are kind of fun to know. When Sharon's teller told her that the money in their bank went to a bigger bank, she was talking about the Federal Reserve. The Federal Reserve banks are places where banks go to bank. But a Federal Reserve Bank is a nicer bank than your bank. When you deposit $100 into your checking account, you're allowed to write checks for $100. When your bank deposits $100 into their account at the Federal Reserve, they're allowed to write checks for $500. This is because of a neat rule called the reserve requirement. At any given time they only have to keep a percentage of the money that they've spent on account. What a deal!

The Federal Reserve can raise or lower the reserve requirement, which changes the amount of money that's in circulation. They also loan money to their banks and they can change the interest rate that they charge, thereby changing the interest rate that your bank would charge you. So, if you haven't figured it out by now, let me explain that the Federal Reserve is a pretty powerful place.

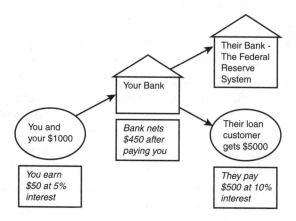

How the Federal Reserve System lets your bank make more money than you thought it did.

How Banks Make Money

Let's think about what this means to you and your money that you deposit in a bank. Let's say that you buy a Certificate of Deposit for $1,000 and the bank will pay you 5 percent interest. That means that in a year you will earn $50. With a 20 percent reserve requirement, your bank can then loan out $5,000 and let's say they charge 10 percent on that money. That means that in a year they will earn $500. I bet you thought they were only making $100 on the $1,000 that you deposited.

So with an extra $450 to spend, you can see where they got the money to build all those safe-looking buildings and hire all those public relations consultants to make you feel comfortable. You can also see why the banking industry has attracted a lot of competition. Through that competition, their profits have been reduced in recent years. Rest assured that no one is pocketing that $450. There are a lot of costs associated with running a bank well.

Our economy is a wonderfully complicated thing—even people who study it have yet to figure out exactly how it works. It isn't your job to understand all the ins and outs of the Federal Reserve System or the stock market or the tax system. But, the more you know, the more you can gain trust in systems that make sense to you. The alternative, of course, is to follow the example of that squirrel: buy some land, bury your food, and work until you die.

The Five Things You Can Do with Money

When you consider all the choices you have regarding investments that might lead to financial security someday, the idea of choosing among those options can be overwhelming. The reality however, is that there are only five things you can do with money and every choice you have is either one of those five things or a combination of two or more of them. When you decide that you'd like to put some money somewhere for retirement, you can easily evaluate your options if you understand which of these five things you're doing.

The five things are ...

1. Keep it as money.
2. Spend it on something.
3. Buy something that you keep.
4. Loan it to someone.
5. Gamble it.

And that's it.

Let me give you some examples. When you put your money into the Social Security System, the government takes it and purchases government bonds with it. Those bonds are a loan that you just made to the Federal Government so that's number 4—*loan it to someone*. When you buy a house that you intend to live in during retirement, that's number 3—*buy something that you keep*. When you give money to a sister-in-law of yours who is starting a construction company, that might be number 5—*gamble it*. Anything that you do with your money can be put into one of these five categories. Let's go through them one at a time and understand what place they have in your retirement planning.

Option 1: Keep It As Money

The first one on the list is 1—*keep it as money*. Now we've already learned that money is not just dollar bills. Money can be electronic impulses at big banks, but it can also be the familiar green stuff. The notion of burying money in the backyard or stuffing it under the mattress has pretty much gone away with fallout shelters and we usually allow our federally insured institutions to hold onto it for us. In a period of inflation, where your money is losing its value, keeping it as money immediately means that you have lost some of it.

Option 2: Spend It on Something

There are reasons to hold money as money and they normally involve needing it to be able to 2—*spend it on something*. This is a category I don't have to explain to most of you. This is what drives your daily living and ongoing stress regarding money. How many years have you looked at your W-2 in January and wondered, "Where did it all go? Why don't I have anything to show for it?" You spend money on taxes to keep our government going, food to feed your children, transportation to get to work, and a vacation from that work.

Option 3: Buy Something You Keep

The next thing you can do with your money is 3—*buy something that you keep*. The store that sells Beanie Baby toys across from my office was doing a jumping business a couple of years ago and we all know people who have the rarest of the rare of those little critters. Maybe you're one of them. They bought them to keep them, they didn't take off the tags, and they bought covers for the tags. They bought them expecting that they would go up in value, and some of them have.

When you buy something that you keep, you either buy it to use it, to earn money off of it, or to sell it some day for a profit. Your house could actually fall into all three of those categories. You might live in it, you might rent it out, and you might sell it someday at a profit. You might buy stock in a company for its income opportunities because the company pays regular dividends or you may buy a stock in a company that you expect to increase in value so you can sell it and make a profit some day.

The future value of any of these items is totally dependent upon whether another human will find value in it someday. In collecting, this is called the Greater Fool theory. If you can find someone that's a greater fool than you, you can sell what you bought for more money and make a profit. If you're the greatest fool, then you'll lose money on the item when you try to sell it.

When we say something will be worth something someday, what we really mean is there will be a person we can find who is willing to buy it at a higher price than we paid. It would be rare that we would expect to sell that item back to the same person that we bought it from. Normally, their interest in it is done and we would need to find a new buyer for the item when we're done with it. This is why markets, whether they be flea markets or stock markets, are so important to our investment returns. They bring people together who may be looking for the type of items that we are looking to sell.

Option 4: Loan It to Someone

The next option you have is 4—*loan it to someone.* When your niece calls you up and says she needs a new muffler and you loan her $150 to get it fixed, that could be a gift (meaning you just spent the money on something—your niece's muffler) or it could be a loan. You could expect to receive the money back someday, with interest or some fee for her use of the money for a period of time. When you put money into a Ginnie Mae Fund, you're loaning your money to homebuyers who will receive that money as a mortgage and you will receive interest because they are paying interest on their mortgage. When you buy a corporate or government bond, you are loaning money to that corporation or government. For instance, Municipal bonds are loans that you make to a city or county, usually for improvements for things like roads and sewers and schools and buildings.

Option 5: Gamble It

And then there's gambling. Legal or illegal, state sponsored or church sponsored, the amount of dollars going into this activity has been consistently growing over the last decade. Some people participate in gambling under the guise of an entertainment expenditure. They know they won't win but they enjoy the time spent trying. Some people engage in gambling under the guise of buying something they intend to keep, like junk investments. They may purchase stocks with only one expectation: that the stock will rise in value whether it should or not.

Many financial strategies incorporate more than one of these options. For instance, life insurance is considered a gamble by some, an expenditure that you use up by others, or something that you buy that you intend to keep, meaning the death benefits. Preferred stock is a combination of buying something and loaning money to someone because it has a guaranteed return paid to you by the company that you purchase the stock in, but it also has an underlying ownership of a part of that company.

Which to Use in Retirement Planning

Thinking about these five things you can do with your money helps you plan your financial strategies for retirement. We've pretty much figured out that you don't want to keep it as money. In an inflationary period, which we usually are in, that means you're losing. After you retire, you'll want to have a portion of your retirement funds in money that you can then spend on your needs each month but the bulk of your money will stay in some other form of investment.

You will either own something that is earning money or going up in value, or you've loaned your money to someone and they're paying you interest. Both of those strategies contain varying levels of risk and that's something that we'll talk more about as we go shopping in the next chapter.

The difference between investing and gambling is very important to grasp. Just because an investment carries a risk, doesn't mean that it's a gamble. Gambling is a situation when the people who have wagered bets will split up the money at the end of the evening and the house scrapes off their portion. So, if a hundred gamblers walk into a casino and a hundred gamblers walk out, collectively when they walk out they will have less money than when they walked in. That's a gamble.

If the same hundred people took their money and invested in a corporation that produced a product that created income and that income is distributed across the hundred people, that's an investment. If the company is brand new and may not succeed, it's a risky investment. There has to be some possibility that there will be a return on everyone's money for it to be an investment. In a gambling situation, there's no possibility that there will be a return for the group.

How Your Government Makes Money

You and your cousins might get together next summer to celebrate your grandparent's 50th wedding anniversary. If you each chip in a hundred bucks, you can buy them a cruise. If each of you goes out and spends a hundred dollars, they'll get several nice gifts, but it won't be a cruise.

But, as you're planning this cruise, one of your cousins loses her job and someone mentions that it wouldn't be fair to ask her to pay the entire hundred dollars given that she's now out of work. And then, someone else mentions that there are a few cousins who make an awful lot of money and maybe they could chip in more. By the time you're done, you're back where you started. You have the amount of money you need for the cruise, but different cousins have paid different amounts.

Then someone mentions that your grandparents have never been on a cruise and that your grandmother probably wouldn't like it. Someone declares, "Oh, it will be good for her. She needs to get out and see some of the world." When she gets this gift, she can certainly decide if she doesn't want to go.

The Complexity of Government

This is a small sample of how governments work. The officials determine a funding strategy, sometimes based on ability to pay, and then they determine what goods and services they're going to purchase for the public. Then the public usually has some options to use the services or not. Much of the cost of government is hidden. For example, right now a great deal of our taxes go to pay interest on debt that we've accumulated because we've overspent on our government programs in previous years. Other monies go to help people who are in need. A chunk goes to support our national defense and help countries overseas.

I bet you couldn't name for me all the levels of government that tax you in some way. Some of them are coming out of your paycheck. Some of them are being paid through your gasoline purchases and other products with taxes built in. Some of them send you a bill, like your property taxes, and some of them make you fill out very complicated forms to determine how much is your share to pay.

On the chart that you filled out in Chapter 3, "A Balancing Act," which projects your expenses through your retirement periods, taxes are in there as withholdings or bills in your current budget. When you're retired, you may not have your taxes withheld. You may have to send them in as estimates or write a check at the end of the year with your return.

The government sometimes gives you an option of paying tax now or paying tax later. These options are applied to different types of investments and create what are called tax deferrals and tax exemptions. The two most popular types of tax options that allow a tax deferral are Individual Retirement Accounts and 401(k) plans. These are not investments by themselves. You will pick an investment that you like and then the Individual Retirement Account (IRA) or 401(k) status will be given to it by a separate document, which qualifies it for this special tax deferral. Some investments are automatically tax exempt like municipal bonds, which we now know are loans to your local government, and they are not taxed by your federal government. Since income taxes take the biggest chunk out of our budget of all the taxes we pay, let's look at those a little more closely.

Average vs. Marginal Tax Rates

Let's work through an example together. Cindy earns $40,000 a year as an administrative assistant. Her income tax bill last year was $5,700. Doing the math that means that her average tax rate, if we divide $40,000 by $5,700, we get 7 percent. But if Cindy makes another $1,000, she'll be taxed an additional $280. If we divide $280 into $1,000, we see that her marginal tax rate is 28 percent.

Average vs. Marginal Tax Brackets

First, I'd like you to understand the difference between your average tax rate and your marginal tax rate. You can calculate your own marginal tax rate by pretending that you make an extra $1,000 and go back to your tax chart, or your tax software, or your tax preparer and ask the question, "What would my income tax be if I made $1,000 more?" See how much more tax you would pay, divide that into $1,000 and you have your marginal rate. So, simply put, the marginal rate is the amount of tax you pay on the next dollar you make. Recently, Congress made this a little more complicated by passing the Economic Growth & Tax Relief Reconciliation Act of 2001. The tax brackets above 15 percent will continue to ratchet down until 2006. These new levels are only good until 2010, when Congress will have to take action to have them remain in place.

The following chart helps you see how the different marginal rates are applied. Your average rate is the amount of tax you've paid on the average over all the dollars you make. And that's always going to be lower than your marginal rate because you don't pay tax on the first several thousand dollars of income, due to the exemptions and deductions that are allowed in the tax laws. The marginal rate is the rate that you want to think about when you decide whether you want to pay tax now or pay tax later.

Tax Brackets

Tax Rate	Single	Head of Household	Married Jointly	Married Separately
0% on first	$2,900	$2,900	$5,800	$2,900
0% on next	$0	$2,900 × no. of dependents	$2,900 × no. of dependents	$2,900 × no. of dependents
0% on standard deductions *or* itemized deductions	$4,550 Individually calculated	$6,550** Individually calculated	$7,600 Individually calculated	$3,800 Individually calculated

continues

Tax Brackets (continued)

Tax Rate	Single	Head of Household	Married Jointly	Married Separately
10% on next	$6,000	$10,000	$12,000	$6,000
15% on next	$27,050	$36,250	$45,200**	$22,600
28 to 25%* on next	$38,500	$57,400	$64,050	$32,025
31 to 28%* on next	$71,200	$58,000	$57,250	$28,625
36 to 33%* on next	$160,600	$145,700	$130,850	$65,425
39.6 to 35%* on the rest				

Note: The changes on the last four tax brackets will phase in between 2001 and 2006.

**These numbers will be adjusted gradually until 2009 to eliminate the "marriage penalty."*

As you pick through your own issues with the concept of trust, you'll discover what makes you uncomfortable, what causes you concern, and what keeps you awake at night. You'll need to balance that against the notion that you have to trust other humans in order to retire. To be very blunt about it, humans don't make very good squirrels.

The Bottom Line

Did I get you thinking about your own ability to trust? Are you more or less suspicious now? Do you see why you have been making the investment decisions you have? Keep these thoughts with you as you learn more about the choices you have ahead of you.

Ten years after working her dream job at an engineering firm in New York City, Julia had botched a couple of serious relationships. The long hours and sporadic travel of her job usually got in the way. She was on the partnership track at her firm and was being given bigger and more important assignments.

She had opened a brokerage account at a place that her best friend had recommended. She liked the broker well enough and bought a couple of things that he recommended, but she never saw herself as an investor. Her student loans were almost paid off and she was beginning to think about buying a co-op. Since she was still in debt and she didn't have any dependents, she didn't really need to begin saving up money for anything. She decided that when her student loans were done she would take that money and put it in a savings account to get together the down payment for her apartment. She also had some money that her father managed from her grandmother's estate that she knew she could use for the down payment.

Another ten years and one failed marriage later, she managed to keep custody of most of the furniture in her nice co-op. Since there were no children, her marriage was fairly easy to dissolve and she didn't ask for anything from her husband except the furniture.

Her income was now advancing and her tax preparer suggested that she check into some investments that might help her save some taxes. She thought this was a reasonably good idea but wasn't comfortable explaining to him that she didn't know anything about it.

Most of her net worth was in her home and she was only now starting to think about retirement as she saw some of the partners taking early retirement. It dawned on her one day that 55 was only 15 years away. She had been so focused on her job and relationships that she hadn't taken the time to begin planning her financial security.

Money had been pretty easy up to now, but she was beginning to get the sense that it wouldn't always be that way if she didn't do something to take control. As good as she was at shopping, she wasn't sure her skills would transfer to financial products and she always thought the salespeople were pretty pushy.

Chapter 5

Let's Go Shopping

You know the exact rack that has the bargains, you go to your size, check the price tags, look for flaws and you're good to go. And you take it back if it doesn't fit. We're going shopping now for financial products, and you will do the same thing you've always been good at—find the deals and meet your needs.

At Your Benefits Department

Depending upon where you work, your benefits department could be anything from your boss's wife to an Internet-based, high-tech database with tutorials to walk you through all the various choices that you have. The benefits directors at the companies around the country are going to love me for saying this. My first suggestion is that you give them a call and you offer to take them to lunch. Spend an hour with them and ask the question, "What is it that nobody around here understands that you think is important to know?" Then, just listen to their answer.

They may have the most wonderful insight into the importance of your benefits package that no one's bothered to share with you. They're generally not allowed to be giving you advice or making your choices for you. They can, however, explain from the company's perspective, what's available to you and what sort of benefits and consequences there are with picking each of the choices.

As you familiarize yourself with the various forms of income compensation or group purchasing benefits that your company is offering you, you may find that a lot of it is not really of any interest to you. When we talk about retirement planning, most of the benefits that are offered become important in one way or another. Saving money on your health insurance premium, for instance, might free up more money to allow you to increase your 401(k) plan contribution. Or increasing your disability bene-fit might guarantee that the plan that you put into place would not be thwarted by a sudden disability.

Remember: It's Your Retirement Plan, Not Your Employer's

Don't assume that because your employer has purchased a prod-uct on your behalf, using their group purchasing power, that you're getting a deal. Think of them as one place to go shopping for the services and the products that will meet your needs. Compare those products to services and products available else-where.

For example, if you're under 40, it's possible that your group life insurance benefit will be more expensive than a term life insur-ance product that you might buy from your insurance agent down the street. You won't know until you ask. It's also possible that you may need more life insurance than what your employer has made available for you to purchase. In this case, you need to combine insurance policies available at your employer with insur-ance that you purchase elsewhere.

If I were to put my finger on the biggest mistake that workers make in retirement planning, it's relying on their employer to make the best decisions for them. Most people that I've met in the last 20 years have no retirement plan other than what their employer had put into place.

We become outraged when our employer chooses a Health Maintenance Organization that doesn't reimburse our doctor for services. We want full choice as consumers of our medical care. We don't seem to have the same anger when it comes to our retirement planning. If our employer has chosen a structure for our retirement plan that isn't meeting our needs, we tend to roll over and play dead, rather than take our business elsewhere.

It's All Your Money Paying for It

So you've met someone in the benefits department that you feel comfortable asking questions of and you've looked at all the things that they have to sell. Some of them, obviously, will be very low cost because "the company" is paying a portion of the cost.

But don't think for a minute that's anybody's money but yours that is paying the rest of it. Your employer has a budget for what it costs to get your job done. Part of that budget they expend in cash on you by paying you your gross income, withholding your taxes, and paying their employer taxes on top of that. Part of it they spend on in-kind benefits, like the holiday party, and some of them they share the costs of goods and services that they hope you will value.

Rise of Health Insurance Costs

From 1940 to 1980, the cost of health insurance increased 10 times as a percentage of the average household's budget. From 1980 to 2000, it grew another 3 times.

Employees who have worked for companies that share the cost of their health insurance would probably be shocked to know what the real cost is running. I still see people who believe that their health insurance costs $20 a week because that's what they see come out of their check. When they go back and ask their benefits department and find out that it actually costs $100 a week they can initially think that the employer is kicking in $80. Actually, it's the employee's $80 because that's $80 that they're not getting in their gross pay. This is the basis of contract negotiations when unions go to the table to look at compensation packages. Employers are happy to have employees sharing the costs of their benefits because it makes the employee more aware. Studies have found that the employees value things that they're more aware of.

The 401(k) [and 403(b)] Sections of the Internal Revenue Code

This is part of the reason that 401(k) plans have become so popular in our country. Not too long ago employers had two main options for funding the retirement of their employees. They could put money into a plan on a regular basis calculated as a percentage of the employee's income. These were called Defined Contribution Plans.

Or, they could put money into a plan based on an expected benefit from the plan. These were called Defined Benefit Plans. This is the type of plan that most people referred to as a pension. The plans traditionally paid a stated amount at retirement, which might be a percentage of the employee's highest yearly income.

A little over twenty years ago, the code was reinterpreted to allow what we now call 401(k) plans. 401(k), by the way, is the number of a section of the IRS code. Very simply put, all it said was that both employers and employees were allowed to contribute to Defined Contribution Plans. Prior to that point only employers were allowed to contribute. That's it. That's all 401(k) means.

Since then, we've watched an entire industry of 401(k) products evolve. They've been very attractive to employers because they do the job of making employees aware of their benefits. And we have actually come to believe that the matching contribution that the employers deposit is an afterthought.

Actually, it's the reverse. The employer's portion was there first and the employee was allowed to add to it. Over the years the employer's portion has diminished, sometimes to as low as 2 percent and the employees are funding the majority of the plans.

When 401(k) plans first got started, many of the options were limited to purchasing your own company's stock. In the mid 1990s the rules were changed and employers were required to offer more investment options for employees. Because of employee demand and some liability issues, the market has reacted to allow employers to offer sometimes thousands of mutual fund choices to their employees.

Types of Mutual Funds Available in 401(k) Plans

Common Name of Fund	You are	You earn	Risk
Money market	Keeping it as cash	Interest	Low
Fixed income	Loaning it to someone	Interest	Low
Balanced	Loaning it to someone buying large companies	Interest Dividends	Low
Flexible portfolio	Loaning and buying, it's up to the fund manager	Interest Dividends	Low
Equity Income	Buying dividend-paying companies	Dividends and Capital Gains	Med
Option Income	Buying dividend-paying companies and options	Dividends	Med
Index	Buying companies listed in a certain index	Dividends and Capital Gains	Med
Growth and income	Buying large dividend-paying companies	Dividends and Capital Gains	Med
Growth	Buying mid and large companies	Capital Gains	Med
Socially conscious	Buying companies that behave a certain way	Dividends and Capital Gains	Med

continues

Types of Mutual Funds Available in 401(k) Plans (continued)

Common Name of Fund	You are	You earn	Risk
Small-company growth funds	Buying small companies	Capital Gains	High
Aggressive Growth	Buying small, emerging companies	Capital Gains	High
Foreign stock funds	Buying non-U.S. companies	Dividends and Capital Gains	High

Keeping the IRS Happy Shouldn't Be Your Goal

Remember when we wanted to send Grandma on that cruise? I wonder where the government is sending us this time? If we look behind the motivation of this tax code, we'll see a government that is not interested in being our sole source of support when we retire. So, by giving a tax benefit to working people, they might get us to save more for our retirement. Not a bad reason.

In the changes made to the tax law in 2001, Congress increased from $2000 the amount you can contribute to your retirement funds tax-deferred (see the following table).

Year	Maximum IRA Contribution	Maximum 401(k)/ 403(b) Contribution
2002	$3,000	$11,000
2003	$3,000	$12,000
2004	$3,000	$13,000
2005	$4,000	$14,000
2006	$4,000	$15,000
2007	$4,000	$15,000
2008	$5,000	$15,000
2009 and after	Both will be raised by inflation rate	

In addition, those over 50 will be allowed "catch-up" contributions each year in excess of these amounts. By 2006, $5,000 will be allowed for 401(k) plans and $1,000 for IRA accounts.

One of the problems that the IRS is concerned about with 401(k) plans is that the owners, officers, and highly paid employees of a company will get all the benefit and that the lower paid employees will get much less of a benefit from the plan. So to prevent 401(k) plans from being merely a tax shelter for the rich, the IRS has imposed strict standards on the participation in the plan. Highly paid consultants are calculating madly the participation rates of different levels of employees to make sure it is not only the top dogs that are using it.

What this really means is that if you are a high-earning person, sometimes your contribution level will be limited so that the plan does not become top heavy. If you're a lower-earning employee, often you will be encouraged to participate more to help balance out the plan. Even though I applaud the efforts of the plan administrators to make sure the plan is within the law and to make sure it remains in place for you to enjoy, that should not be your sole criteria for determining your participation level. If the plan makes sense for you and the investments make sense for you and the tax status of those investments make sense for you, then it's a wonderfully convenient and smart way to save for retirement. If, however, you look at your situation, your tax deferral needs, your investment strategy preferences and you find your plan doesn't meet those needs, please don't feel coerced into participating just to meet the overall needs of the plan.

Individual Retirement Account Deductibility Limits

If you are an active participant of a retirement plan you can make a deposit into an IRA each year but the deposit will not be tax-deferred if you earn over:

Single	$42,000
Head of household	$42,000
Married filing jointly	$62,000
Married filing separately	$10,000

For income levels $10,000 below these amounts, there is a full deduction. Between the amounts, there is a graduated deduction. Earnings on the IRA account are tax-deferred. Roth IRA's are available for individuals earning up to $110,000 and couples up to $160,000.

Portability Matters More Than It Used To

Even though the benefits package available at your employer is designed to help keep you working there, the likelihood of you remaining at your current employer until retirement is going down each year. More workers are changing jobs more frequently than ever before. One of the things to keep in mind as you shop at your benefits department is what we call portability. If you purchase a product, especially an insurance product, can you take it with you and if you take it with you, what will the cost be? Products such as long-term care insurance may look very affordable at your employer and may be portable at no change or very slight change in cost. But, products such as health insurance may be affordable while you're an employee and then become very expensive as you take it with you because you're now officially paying the full cost.

If you're looking for an insurance product, whether it's life insurance, disability insurance, long-term care, car insurance, or some other product that is offered by your benefits department and you believe that you will need to carry this insurance beyond the time that you will likely be working for this employer, then this issue would be very important to you. You might be better off shopping at your insurance agent, bank, or stockbroker. So the bottom line is, as you collect information from your benefits department, think of them as another place to shop and compare the products, the prices, and the portability with products available at the other locations we're going to visit in this chapter.

At Your Insurance Agent

Let me see a show of hands: How many of you love your insurance agent? Well, I was one once, many years ago, and I didn't feel very loved. There is a general aura of suspicion that surrounds insurance agents in our country. Most of them are pretty hard-working, honest folks who have a pretty hard job.

In our sales training we were taught that we had to call 100 people to get 10 appointments to make 3 people interested to make one sale. Knowing this, you can imagine what happens when you pick up the phone to call an insurance agent and say, "Hi, I'd like to come over and talk to you." This just doesn't happen, ever. After the insurance agent figures out that you're not a prankster, you're going to get wonderful treatment. You're going to get to pick the time and the place and the topic.

Here's what you're going to say, "I'm _____ years old and I'm planning to live another _____ years. During that time I will be working for _____ years and while I'm working I will have _____ amount of money to put toward my retirement. Once I'm retired I will need ____ amount of money per month to supplement my other retirement income sources. Can you propose three products that you feel might help me meet those goals? And can you look at the insurance and investment products that I have purchased on my own and through my employer to determine if I'm getting the best value for my money?"

Now you've probably figured out that this question is sort of like asking a three-year-old if they want a cookie. You know what the answer will be; the problem will be keeping them from wanting another one. If the agent can't answer those questions for you in a way that sounds to you like they're answering the questions, then explain that to them. Tell them, "You're not answering my questions. Would you like to try again?" If they have been trained to give a specific sale's pitch on a specific product and they can't answer your specific questions, move on. Find someone who can.

Remember that no one's going to turn you down for an appointment. The only risk is that they won't come prepared. Don't waste any more time than you must to determine whether or not they're ready to answer your questions. This is important because you're going to have more questions over the years, and you need to feel confident that the person selling you products is ready to answer them.

Standard Product-Types Available from Insurance Companies

The following are standard product-types available from insurance companies:

❖ Whole life insurance: An insurance contract with an extra premium charged in early years to allow the premium to stay level in later years. The "extra" premium builds up a cash value that can be cashed out once your need for the insurance has passed.

❖ Universal life insurance: Similar to whole life insurance except that the "extra" premium is invested in slightly higher-earning investments.

❖ Fixed annuities: A contract where you pay the insurance company a lump sum (or monthly payments) and they pay you back in monthly payments, guaranteed for life.

❖ Variable annuities: Similar to a fixed annuity except that your money is invested in slightly higher-earning investments.

One of the things that we have going for us is that insurance products are regulated by the state insurance commissioners. We haven't had a crisis in the insurance industry (like the Savings and Loan industry saw in the 1980s) since 1860. In 1860, many of the insurance companies were headquartered in New York and there was a major scandal, which brought down many companies. In reaction to that, the New York legislature enacted some strict guidelines to secure the assets of policyholders in the remaining insurance companies.

Many companies form subsidiaries to do business in New York that have to follow the strict New York guidelines. This allows the parent company to do business in all states but New York. You can find this out by going to the library or going to the Web site of *A.M. Best Company. A.M. Best* rates insurance companies and gives us lots of wonderful information to be able to compare one company to the next. Their books will tell you the size and financial strength of the company you are considering.

The other source that you have for impartial information is your state insurance commissioner. Most insurance commissioners have consumer hotlines and fact sheets available at little or no cost to citizens of that state that will help you compare/contrast different policies of companies doing business in that state. They can also tell you if that company has been under any investigation or is under any sanction for violating the state insurance laws.

Your agent will be important as your primary contact with your insurance product, but the company behind the agent is also going to be important, especially if it's the type of insurance that will require multiple claims or ongoing interaction with the company. For instance, a life insurance product has one claim, if that, and you're done. But a disability product or a health insurance product may have multiple claims. An annuity will have monthly checks coming to you.

Drive-Thru Claim Service

When my son was five, he announced one day that he had banks and taxes pretty much figured out, but this insurance thing was confusing him. "Where, exactly, is the money in my life insurance policy?" he wanted to know. "Milwaukee," I answered. "So when the ambulance takes me away, I should tell them to take me to Milwaukee?"

Unless you're five, you probably wouldn't care if your life insurance company has a drive-thru claim service. But you may want your car insurance company to have one.

With the advent of telephone and Internet shopping for insurance products, you may like the anonymity of that service, not having to sit face-to-face with an insurance agent. Or you may prefer more personalized service and someone you can get to know. If you get to the end of this book and continue your investigation into your financial future, you can save some money in commissions and fees by skipping the salesperson. But, if you are not likely to finish this book, and you would prefer an expert to do some of the calculations, the money you spend on fees or commissions will be well worth it to build a good plan and keep you moving toward retirement security.

At Your Bank

Used to be, if it looked like a bank, walked like a bank and quacked like a bank, it was (you guessed it) a bank! But no more. In 1999, Congress repealed the Depression-era Glass-Steagall Act and threw in some swans, geese, and other feathered friends. Banks can now offer a wide range of financial services, competing with our friends in the insurance and investment industries.

The quickest way to accomplish this was through strategic partnerships, alliances, mergers and anything else the attorneys could dream up to be able to move on this the minute the president's signature hit the bill. I got a letter postmarked that exact day (my birthday!) explaining that my bank now offered insurance through a very respected company. Now you know they hadn't just woken up that morning and read the paper and decided to go into the insurance business. They had been waiting for this opportunity for *years*. It's the old "If you can't beat 'em, join 'em" strategy.

Standard Products Available at Banks

❖ Savings accounts: Deposit accounts that you can make frequent withdrawals from, usually paying interest equal to the inflation rate.

❖ Certificates of deposit: Deposit accounts that you can cash in at specific dates in the future, without a penalty, usually paying marginally higher rates than savings accounts.

❖ Money market funds: A mutual fund account that buys different cash equivalents and may require higher initial deposit and limited withdrawals.

The banks of our childhood are gone. The lollipops went out the door with liability lawsuits, the fallout shelters are bare, and the products are very different. They are attempting to be your one stop financial product center. And they've got a drive thru! And a Web site! And nice salespeople, too!

Remember the questions we learned to ask insurance agents:

"I'm _____ years old and I'm planning to live another _____ years. During that time I will be working for _____ years and while I'm working I will have _____ amount of money to put toward my retirement. Once I'm retired I will need ____ amount of money per month to supplement my other retirement income sources. Can you propose three products that you feel might help me meet those goals? And can you look at the insurance and investment products that I have purchased on my own and through my employer to determine if I'm getting the best value for my money?"

Ask the same questions of your banker. But don't expect to be able to pick the time and place, in most situations. I have had my office across the street from my bank for twelve years. No one has ever walked across the street to say hello, even though I watch them walk past me to get to the local carryout. They seem to think they're like the one pizza place in town that doesn't deliver, but doesn't have to.

Or maybe I'm not their market. I'm female, married with kids, 40-something, working and still wondering if I get to retire someday. You can find out if you are in your bank's marketing plan with a simple phone call. Then the same rules apply. If they are not answering your questions, tell them. If they still don't answer them, move on.

At Your Stockbroker

What a difference a Web makes! When the major stockbrokerage firms moved onto the Internet as a means to marketing their products, a whole new world opened up for us. The stockbrokers of the past were represented by very aggressive salespeople who were all after the top 10 percent of the investing public. Not you and me, for sure. Oh, those people still exist and they are still after the same market. But you have access to their services without being a big fish.

They have put salespeople in the lobbies of banks that they have formed marketing partnerships with. They have allowed you to purchase shares of stock and other investments through the mail and online without a salesperson.

The following are standard products available at stockbrokers:

- ❖ Cash Products: Certificates of Deposit, Money Markets, and Checking services
- ❖ Stocks: Pieces of companies, can be big, small, new or old, successful or in trouble
- ❖ Bonds: Loans to companies or governments, can be short or long term, can be tax-exempt
- ❖ Mutual Funds: Cash, bond or stock investments packaged for you and managed by a management company
- ❖ Insurance: Death benefit and annuity policies

What we didn't know is that they have been selling life insurance products, like annuities, for a long time. And they have banking products, like money markets and CDs. The only difference was who they were selling to. Not you. But that is changing and they want your business now. They have figured out that you earn money, live longer and control more personal wealth than men. So use it. Ask your questions:

"I'm _____ years old and I'm planning to live another _____ years. During that time I will be working for _____ years and while I'm working I will have _____ amount of money to put toward my retirement. Once I'm retired I will need ____ amount of money to supplement my other retirement income sources. Can you propose three products that you feel might help me meet those goals? And can you look at the insurance and investment products that I have purchased on my own and through my employer to determine if I'm getting the best value for my money?"

Same rules. You are going to be really good at this by the time you're done. Use your shopping skills and good sense about people. You've heard an insurance agent, banker, and stockbroker all answer the same question. What was different? What pushed your buttons? What made you want to learn more? How are each of them earning their money? How do they charge you for their services? Which is most cost-effective for your situation?

These three types of financial companies used to be very different, with different purposes in your life. The lines are getting very fuzzy. Some distinct differences remain and you will learn them as you talk to all three. For example, your banker will talk 'till sundown about the FDIC insurance on your bank accounts. The stockbroker will fail to mention that, but will show you CD rates higher than banks. The insurance company will emphasize their size and strength as an insurer. The stockbroker will tell you how many trades they handle. They can't really break away from their old sales pitches. So, see what makes a difference to you. But make sure it is you making the decision, not your father's lectures from 40 years ago. Things have changed.

The Bottom Line

When it's important, you take your time and make sure it fits just right. The products you buy to put into your retirement plan are about as important as any you will ever buy. Make sure they fit, and that you know how to care for them.

---

t was the proudest moment of Christina's life. She was watching her baby walk across the stage to get his degree. His older brother and sister had walked similar stages before him, but this was different. He was her youngest and had always been closest to her. As she fought back her tears, she didn't know if she was crying because she was happy or sad. He was a wonderful young man with tremendous opportunities ahead of him. She knew that she had done her job well. That was the problem: She knew her job was done. Oh, not her real job, the one she went to every morning. But this job, the important one, the one her heart was in. It would probably be several years before any of her children would find it convenient to give her grandchildren, and she could already feel the void.

Her husband was distant at the graduation party. He didn't deal with her very well when she was emotional. When her son left to join all of his buddies at their favorite hangout, she and her husband went back to their hotel room. She lay awake well into the night, joyous and grieving at the same time.

A week later she came home from work and unlocked the door quickly as the phone was ringing. Her son called every day to update her on his job and apartment search. As she talked to him, she sorted through the mail she had grabbed out of the mailbox on the way in.

There was a very official looking letter from the local courts addressed to her. As she realized what she was looking at, her son's words became distant. She looked across the room—the golf trophies were gone from the corner cupboard. She dropped the phone and began to sob. This couldn't be happening to her...

Chapter 6

Putting Together Your Plan

Retirement plans have a lot of assumptions, such as inflation, interest rates, budgets, and longevity. You are about to find out if your assumptions work together to give you a solid retirement plan.

What Do You Know?

I wish I had a dollar for every time someone has said to me, "Well, you just can't plan because you don't know what's going to happen." Actually, it's the opposite. You have to plan *because* you don't know what's going to happen. The best plan will accept change as a given and allow you the flexibility to live through it.

At the beginning of this book I asked you to pick the year you're going to die. That's a pretty weird concept because generally we don't do that, at least not thirty years in advance. And then I asked you to pick the day you're going to enter Low Retirement, the day that you're going to enter High Retirement, and the day that you're going to be able to increase your savings level. It's not important whether you're right or wrong about these dates.

What's important is that you've chosen them to be able to create a plan. Once we work through this plan with one set of variables, then you'll be able to go back and put in any variables you want.

One word of caution before we continue: There are certain times in people's lives where planning is not a good idea. Making changes and tackling big decisions need to take second place to a more important process. If you have just lost someone close to you; or like Christina, are grieving for the loss of your role as a mother or wife, give yourself time to get through that.

Too many times women do not think about these important decisions until their husband dies or leaves, when they realize that they really do need to plan for their own future. But my caution is to not do it right away. Most things will wait weeks, or even months, for you to become calm and confident in your decision-making ability. You are more vulnerable during this time to trust people you shouldn't and spend money you don't have in an attempt to feel some control over something. Your only job during these periods of your life is to process your grief and return to a normal life. Just make lists of things that you need to do when you get there, including finishing this book.

Present Value Calculations

Well, let's all take a deep breath and get started. The most important thing we need to get out of the way is a discussion about a tremendously powerful mathematical concept called *present value*. This is the rabbit in the financial planner's magical hat. I'm going to teach it to you because a) it really is fun once you understand it; b) I know you're smart enough to get it; and c) it is the key to understanding your retirement plan.

There are three ways you can calculate present value. The first is by using a table like the following. The second is by using a special type of calculator that has keys with the letters "n," "i," "PV," "PMT," and "FV." The third way is to use a computer spreadsheet program like Microsoft Excel. I must confess, I lied; there is a fourth. You can do it by hand, but they locked up the last guy who actually knew how.

Future Value Table for a Lump Sum

Value of $100 at Each (i) Interest Rate After (n) Periods

Rate:	1%	2%	3%	4%	5%	6%	7%	8%	9%
Number of Periods									
1	$101	$102	$103	$104	$105	$106	$107	$108	$109
2	$102	$104	$106	$108	$110	$112	$114	$117	$119
3	$103	$106	$109	$112	$116	$119	$123	$126	$130
4	$104	$108	$113	$117	$122	$126	$131	$136	$141
5	$105	$110	$116	$122	$128	$134	$140	$147	$154
6	$106	$113	$119	$127	$134	$142	$150	$159	$168
7	$107	$115	$123	$132	$141	$150	$161	$171	$183
8	$108	$117	$127	$137	$148	$159	$172	$185	$199
9	$109	$120	$130	$142	$155	$169	$184	$200	$217
10	$110	$122	$134	$148	$163	$179	$197	$216	$237
15	$116	$135	$156	$180	$208	$240	$276	$317	$364
20	$122	$149	$181	$219	$265	$321	$387	$466	$560
25	$128	$164	$209	$267	$339	$429	$543	$685	$862
30	$135	$181	$243	$324	$432	$574	$761	$1,006	$1,327

We're going to start with the chart because I know everyone has that, and then we'll take our skills back to the calculator and the spreadsheet. Start with a simple example. If you put $100 into a savings account at the beginning of the year and it earns 4 percent interest and they only pay interest once a year, you have $104 at the end of the year. Look on the chart for the column with 4 percent. Find the row equal to 1 time period. Follow them down and across and you will find $104.

The variables in this example are:

1. "PV" or Present Value is equal to $100.

2. "n" or Number of time periods is equal to 1.

3. "i" or Interest rate is equal to 4.

And the answer is:

4. "FV" or Future Value is equal to $104.

If you know three of these four items, your chart, calculator, or computer can figure out the other one. So, if I were to ask you, "I put $100 in my saving's account at the beginning of the year and I had $104 at the end of one year, what was my interest rate?" This time you know:

1. "PV" or Present Value is equal to $100.

2. "n" or Number of time periods is equal to 1.

4. "FV" or Future Value is equal to $104.

And you can solve for:

3. "i" or Interest Rate is equal to 4.

Or, if I said to you, "I have $104 in my saving's account, it's been earning 4 percent and it's been there a year, what did I start with?"

2. "n" or Number of time periods is equal to 1.

3. "i" or Interest Rate is equal to 4.

4. "FV" or Future Value is equal to $104.

Therefore, your answer is:

    1. "PV" or Present Value is equal to $100.

You could also understand and figure out that I started with $100. But would you believe that that's all there is to it? And that all these years, the financial planners had you believing that this was difficult.

On our chart the PV (Present Value) is always $100. So if in the above example we changed our deposit to be $200, we would have to multiply our answer by 2, meaning $208 FV (Future Value.)

Interest Rate Warning

Remember that your time period has to match your interest rate. If you are depositing to an account monthly and your interest rate is 6 percent *annually* you need to change one or the other to make them match. Either $1200 at 6 percent *or* $100 at 0.5 percent.

Now, just like most simple things, we can get more complicated if we want to. Let's say that we make five yearly deposits of $100 instead of just one and our money still grows at 4 percent. This is what we call a stream of payments instead of just a present value calculation. So, we're going to add another variable to our calculation: PMT or Ongoing Payment.

This time we know:

    2. "n" or Number of Periods is equal to 5.

    3. "i" or Interest Rate is equal to 4.

    5. "PMT" or Ongoing Payment is equal to $100.

And we can figure out that:

    4. "FV" or Future Value is equal to $541.60.

The second chart, below, helps you see how to get that answer. Just like the first calculation, if we know three of the four variables, we can calculate the fourth.

Future Value Table for Annuity Payments

Value of $100/Period at Each (i) Interest Rate After (n) Periods

Rate:	1%	2%	3%	4%	5%	6%	7%	8%	9%	10%
Number of Periods										
1	$100	$100	$100	$100	$100	$100	$100	$100	$100	$100
2	$201	$202	$203	$204	$205	$206	$207	$208	$209	$210
3	$303	$306	$309	$312	$315	$318	$321	$325	$328	$331
4	$406	$412	$418	$425	$431	$437	$444	$451	$457	$464
5	$510	$520	$531	$542	$553	$564	$575	$587	$598	$611
6	$615	$631	$647	$663	$680	$698	$715	$734	$752	$772
7	$721	$743	$766	$790	$814	$839	$865	$892	$920	$949
8	$829	$858	$889	$921	$955	$990	$1,026	$1,064	$1,103	$1,144
9	$937	$975	$1,016	$1,058	$1,103	$1,149	$1,198	$1,249	$1,302	$1,358
10	$1,046	$1,095	$1,146	$1,201	$1,258	$1,318	$1,382	$1,449	$1,519	$1,594
15	$1,610	$1,729	$1,860	$2,002	$2,158	$2,328	$2,513	$2,715	$2,936	$3,177
20	$2,202	$2,430	$2,687	$2,978	$3,307	$3,679	$4,100	$4,576	$5,116	$5,727
25	$2,824	$3,203	$3,646	$4,165	$4,773	$5,486	$6,325	$7,311	$8,470	$9,835
30	$3,478	$4,057	$4,758	$5,608	$6,644	$7,906	$9,446	$11,328	$13,631	$16,449

Next, we'll try the financial calculator. Let's do the calculation of the savings of $100 for five years at 4 percent.

1. **Clear**
2. **100 PMT**   Enters the Ongoing Payment as $100
3. **4 i**   Enters the Interest Rate as 4 percent
4. **5 n**   Enters the Number of Periods as 5
5. **FV**   Gives you the Future Value result of –$541.60

The answer shows as –$541.60 because we entered the payment as positive. These calculators show you the answer as negative, the money coming back to you. If you enter the payment as negative, the answer comes back positive. Please don't ask me why.

It all boils down to the old saying, "A bird in the hand is worth two in the bush." These formulas just tell you why.

Now, let's try the most fun way—using Excel. To do this, follow these steps:

1. Click **Start, Programs, Microsoft Excel.** You'll be looking at a blank spreadsheet.
2. On the first toolbar of icons, across the top, you should see a fancy fx. This is the function key. Click it. A dialog box appears that gives you a choice of different types of functions.
3. Choose **Financial.** Under Function Name, you'll now see a list starting with "DB," "DDB," "FV," and so on. The five variables that we've been working with are there, too:
    1. "PV"—Present Value
    2. "NPER"—Number of Periods ("n" above)
    3. "RATE"—Interest Rate ("i" above)
    4. "FV"—Future Value
    5. "PMT"—Payment Amount
4. To decide which function will do what you want, click the item you don't know, the item you are trying to figure out.

Let's repeat the problem we just solved on the calculator. We would choose FV—Future Value, because that is what we want to find out. Click **OK.**

5. Up pops a dialogue box with labels that should begin to look very familiar. It is asking us for:

3. "RATE"—Interest Rate. Enter as **.04** (not 4).

2. "NPER"—Number of Periods. Enter as **5.**

5. "PMT"—Payment Amount. Enter as **100.**

The answer appears just as it did in the calculator: –$541.60. Notice that it also has a place for PV. This would be used if you were calculating the FV of a single sum, instead of a stream of payments.

Using Present Value to Calculate Debt Payments

If I know that I borrow $3000 for a vacation, I want to pay it off in two years, and my interest is 10 percent, then I could ask the question, "What is my payment?" A Present Value Table would help me figure that out. When you play with this enough, you realize that calculating savings or your end result over a number of years of saving, is really just the opposite of calculating a debt payment on money that you borrowed out at the beginning.

With the savings calculation, your variables will be:

❖ PMT—your payment

❖ RATE or *i*—your interest rate

❖ NPER or *n*—your number of periods

❖ FV—your future value, what you have left at the end

With a loan calculation your variables will be:

❖ PMT—your payment

❖ RATE or *i*—your interest rate

❖ NPER or *n*—your number of periods

❖ PV—your present value, which is what you borrow at the beginning

Look at the following table and find the payment for a loan at 10 percent for 3 years. The amount on the chart is $32. Since this is for a loan of $1000, we have to multiply it by 3 to get the payment for a $3000 loan. My payment will be $96.

Using the calculator, your entries would be:

1. **Clear**
2. **3000 PV** Enters the amount of the loan as $3000
3. **10 g i** Enters the Interest Rate as 10 percent (.8 percent monthly)
4. **3 g n** Enters the Number of Periods as 3 (36 months)
5. **PMT** Gives you the Payment result of –$96.80

Using Excel, your entries would be:

1. fx
2. Choose **Financial**
3. Choose **PMT**
4. Click **OK**
5. Enter **.10/12** into Rate box
6. Enter **36** into NPER box
7. Enter **3000** into PV box
8. Click **OK**

Retirement Planning Using Present Value

Now, let me share with you an example of why knowing how to do this is so powerful. I'm not recommending this as a planning tool but ... let's assume that you play the lottery today. You win and a gentleman calls from the lottery commission to explain that you have two options. You can take $100,000 today or you can have 10 payments of $11,000, one a year for the next 10 years. Now, since I know you got out of the third grade, you know that 10 times $11,000 is $110,000, which is more than $100,000.

With your new skills at calculating present value, you can determine exactly how much that stream of payments is worth, compared to the lump sum that you can receive today. If you take $11,000 as your payment and $100,000 as your present value and 10 as your number of periods, you'll see that the interest on that stream of payments is only 1.8 percent. You might say to yourself, "Well, I can make more than 1.8 percent on my money. So, I would be better off taking the $100,000 now and investing it because then I would get more than $11,000 a year for the next 10 years if I were to draw out money from my investment."

This is the ultimate strategy in comparing apples and apples. You have to pick a point in time that you compare various investments, stream of payments, savings, or whatever you're comparing. In order to change a stream of payments into a fixed amount, you use this calculation. The Present Value is the total amount that a series of future payments is worth today at a particular interest rate. Sometimes you're given this type of option from a retirement plan. You might be able to take a lump sum, or you might be able to take a certain number of payments for a certain number of years, or you might be able to take a lower payment for a longer period of time. If you reduce the stream of payments back to their present value, using an interest rate that you believe you can earn on your money, then you can compare them to the lump sum option that you've been given.

Designing a retirement plan means first calculating the future value of your current deposits to various savings' programs. Then, you will calculate the present value of the stream of payments that you will need to supplement your income at retirement. When you get these two numbers to match, you're done. I'm going to take my time explaining what I just said and we'll do it until you get it, because it's very important. It answers the two most important mysteries of retirement planning:

❖ How much will I have?

❖ How much will I need?

But first, we're going to go back to that notion that I told you a few chapters ago that you would understand more when you got a lot older—inflation. You're at least a couple of hours older now, which is about as long as it took you to learn the rest of the stuff in fourth grade, too! So, I think you're ready. The way I'm going to explain this isn't exactly accurate, but this is the way that I think it will make the most sense to you and will bring you closest to feeling confident to be able to do this on your own. And, since we're making up most of this anyway, I'm happy to get you close to your target.

Let's go back to the notion that inflation is a decrease in the value of your money. And let's assume that inflation averages 3 percent over time in the United States' economy. If you have a mutual fund that earned 15 percent last year, the first 3 percent of it was not due to the wonderful fund manager or the irrational people on the floor of the stock exchange who ran the price up. It was due to the general decrease in the value of your money. So, you had a *real return* of 12 percent. On paper it looked like 15 percent. Likewise, if you had an investment that lost 5 percent this year, it actually lost 8 percent and if you had an investment that earned 3 percent, you broke even. So get used to making an automatic adjustment in your brain in the interest rate for inflation. When you do this, then you don't have to make an adjustment for inflation in the answer. This is sort of like that old bathroom scale that always tells you that you weigh three pounds less than you do. It makes you feel good but you know, during your honest moments, that you really weigh three pounds more.

For example, your stockbroker might say, "I can sell you this wonderful investment that is projected to earn you 12 percent over the next 20 years," and he tells you that your $100 a month will return you $99,000 in 20 years. But that's not dollars that you know today because there's going to be 3 percent inflation during that time period. So if you were to ask him then to change his projection and reduce that to 9 percent, you would see a number like $67,000. Now, this would be the purchasing power of that $99,000 in dollars that you know today. So the actual projection may say $99,000, but it will only buy $67,000 worth of stuff.

The next calculation that complicates things is the income tax that you will have to pay on your investments. As I've explained before, the IRS gets their money one way or the other. You will either be calculating the tax against the money as you put it into your investments or you will be calculating the tax as you take it out of your investments during your retirement period, unless you have funded an investment which is tax exempt.

Tax-Exempt Investment

You'll notice a very strange relationship between the bond rates on tax-exempt bonds and the rates on taxable bonds; the market has a strange way of making these two equal for most taxpayers. For instance, if you pay about a third of your income in income tax, you may find that the taxable rate is about one-third above the tax-exempt rate.

Remember, several chapters ago you calculated your marginal tax rate. Just like we're going to knock off inflation from a projected interest rate, we're also going to knock off your taxes from the projected interest rate. Taking an earlier example of a 12 percent investment, if you are in the 28 percent tax bracket, you would multiply 12 by .28 and that would give you 3.4 percent. So we need to knock about three and a half points off of the twelve. Then subtract the 3 percent inflation. So, if your 12 percent investment is taxable at 28 percent, you'll actually be earning 5.6 percent after income taxes and inflation. If you are in the 15 percent marginal tax bracket: 15 percent of 12 is 1.8 percent, which leaves you with 10.2 percent. Knock off the inflation and you are earning 7.2 percent.

The choice of the interest rate to start with is probably the hardest number that you'll pick in this exercise. But remember, as you learn more and as you talk to more salespeople, you can go back and readjust it for new assumptions. There is a rate that economists agree is a default risk-free rate. This is normally assigned to the rate that the Federal Government pays for money. This would be the rate that you might earn if you purchased a Treasury Bill. Since the Government can print money and has not yet defaulted on any of its obligations, you can be pretty sure that the rate they're paying is the rate that you could earn with no default risk. You would demand a higher return on any investment you make that has any more risk than that. The more the risk, the more you would demand as compensation to take that risk.

So a risk-free return, after taxes (in the 28 percent bracket) and inflation would be:

7 percent × 28 percent (tax bracket) = 2 percent (taxes)

7 percent – 2 percent (taxes) – 3 percent (inflation) = 2 percent after-tax real return

In the 15 percent bracket it looks like this:

7 percent × 15 percent (tax bracket) = 1 percent (taxes)

7 percent – 1 percent (taxes) – 3 percent (inflation) = 3 percent after-tax real return

So any taxable rates of return under 4.5 percent for those in the 28 percent bracket or under 3.5 percent for those in the 15 percent bracket is just breaking even. Unless, of course, inflation happens to be less than 3 percent at that point in time.

Do the Numbers

I promised you that you would be using a calculator in ways that you never dreamed. You now have all the numbers to crunch— the first time through. Remember that you may change them all before you are done. You may have to change them as your circumstances change. Let's gather all the numbers we currently know:

Final List of Variables

	Before Retirement	After Retirement
Interest Rate I Can Achieve	_____%	_____%
× (1 – Marginal Tax Rate)	_____%	_____%
After-Tax Interest Rate	=_____%	=_____%
– Inflation Rate	3%	3%
After-Tax/After Inflation Rate	=_____%	=_____%
	(r1)	(r2)

A _____ Number of Years in Low Savings Period

B _____ Number of Years in High Savings Period

C _____ Amount Saving per Month in Low Savings Period

D _____ Amount Saving per Month in High Savings Period

E _____ Amount I Already Have Saved

F _____ Number of Years in High Retirement Period

G _____ Number of Years in Low Retirement Period

H _____ Amount Needed per Month in High Retirement Period

J _____ Amount Needed per Month in Low Retirement Period

K _____ Amount I Want to Leave in My Estate

Remember that you are going to be contributing to your retirement funds during your Low Savings and High Savings periods, then withdrawing money from those funds during your High Retirement and Low Retirement periods. The turning point is the beginning of your High Retirement period. What we are going to do is use the concept of Present Value to see if what you are saving now will equal what you will spend later. By taking the taxes and inflation off the interest rates before we calculate these two values, we are comparing apples and apples.

Next, you will need to calculate three (FV) Future Value calculations.

1. The (FV) Future Value of your current retirement investments.
2. The (FV) Future Value of your Low Savings contributions.
3. The (FV) Future Value of your High Savings contributions.

How Much Will I Have?

Copy Your Variables from the Last Chart:

r1	A	B	C	D	E
_____	_____	_____	_____	_____	_____

Calculate the Future Value of Your Savings:

L _____ Future Value (FV) of Amount Already Saved

_____ PV = E

_____ NPER = A + B

_____ RATE = r1

M _____ Future Value (FV) of Low Savings Amount

_____ PMT = C × 12

_____ NPER = A + B

_____ RATE = r1

N _____ Future Value (FV) of High Savings Amount

_____ PMT = (D × 12) − (C × 12)

_____ NPER = B

_____ RATE = r1

X _____ Total Amount Available at High Retirement

L + M + N

And finally, you will need to calculate three (PV) Present Value calculations.

1. The (PV) Present Value of the money you would like to leave in your estate (principal that you don't use up.)
2. The (PV) Present Value of your High Retirement additional income needs.
3. The (PV) Present Value of your Low Retirement additional income needs. (This one has two steps because it doesn't bump up against the High Retirement date.)

How Much Will I Need?

Copy Your Variables Here:

r2	F	G	H	J	K
___	___	___	___	___	___

Calculate the Future Value of Your Savings:

P _____ Present Value (PV) of Amount Left in Estate

_____ FV = K

_____ NPER = F + G

_____ RATE = r2

Q _____ Present Value (PV) of High Retirement Amount

_____ PMT = H × 12

_____ NPER = F + G

_____ RATE = r2

R _____ Present Value (PV) of Low Retirement Amount at beginning of Low Retirement Period

_____ PMT = (J × 12) − (H × 12)

_____ NPER = G

_____ RATE = r2

S _____ Present Value (PV) of Low Retirement Amount at beginning of High Retirement Period

_____ FV = S

_____ NPER = F

_____ RATE = r2

Y _____ Total Amount Needed for High and Low Retirement

P + Q + S

What Do You Need to Revise?

Wow! You did it. And now you get to celebrate, or keep working. If the Future Values (X) you calculated are equal to or more than the Present Values (Y) you calculated, you are on your way to a secure retirement. If not, you have some decisions to make.

Let's list the changes that you can control that will move you in the right direction:

❖ Increase the risk you take and the rate of return.

❖ Increase the Low Savings period contribution.

❖ Increase the High Savings period contribution.

❖ Increase the number of years in the High Savings period.

❖ Decrease the High Retirement lifestyle expenditures.

❖ Increase the High Retirement earned income.

❖ Decrease the number of years in the High Retirement period.

Here's a list of things you don't have control over that will help you:

❖ A decrease in your income tax rate.

❖ An earlier death date.

❖ A healthier economy with higher real rates of return.

As you think through the numbers and the options, be aware that as scary as it may look, it's a lot more comfortable to find out now than the day you retire. There is a solution and you will find it. You will automatically run through the easy solutions first and when they don't do the trick, you may assume that you have no power to achieve your goal.

Reasons for Retirement

Sixty-four percent of people surveyed cited accumulated savings as a reason to retire. Fifty-nine percent blamed a decline in health and only 24 percent pointed to reaching a certain age as one of the reasons.
—*National Council on the Aging*

Think through the not-so-easy solutions for a moment. These are the things that automatically pop into your head as things you would never consider. Write them down.

I would never consider _____.

I would never consider _____.

I would never consider _____.

I would never consider _____.

I would never consider _____.

I would never consider _____.

I have heard them all as a financial counselor.

❖ "If you think my kid is going to get student loans, you're crazy."

❖ "I'm not moving, I've worked my entire life to pay off this house."

❖ "Bankruptcy is *out of the question!*"

❖ "I refuse to get a part-time job. I have health issues."

The funny part is that, most of the time, I haven't even whispered the idea and they are attacking me as though I just ordered them to do it.

Okay, you've got your list of undesirable options. Now fill in the blank:

Before I'd do anything on the list above, I'd do

_____.

And there you have it, your solution! Plug it into the formulas and see what impact it has. If it doesn't get you there, do it again. What's the next thing you'd try before having to resort to anything on your undesirable list?

You may not arrive at all your solutions right this minute. They may come with additional shopping trips or conversations with yourself to clarify your values and your vision of retirement. These values and visions may very well change between now and your High Retirement date. Pick a day each year to meet with your plan and check out your earlier assumptions. Make revisions as necessary and write down your new plan. Then put it away for a year and see if it makes sense next year. As you get closer to your High Retirement date, you will want to look at it a little more often.

The Bottom Line

It all boils down to two numbers: what you have and what you need. Getting to those two numbers takes a lot of guessing, number crunching and courage. When you get them to equal each other, you have a plan.

Part 2

Preparing for Retirement

It's getting closer. You can see it coming, but you're still not feeling ready. Now you're probably wondering: Did I save enough? How can I catch up now? What do I need to do with all my insurance products? What do I have to do to get signed up for Medicare and Social Security? With one of the most important transitions of your life just around the corner, you have a lot of things on your mind. We'll do some last minute course corrections and make sure you are ready for this exciting time.

Susan married her high school sweetheart at 17. He was being shipped out for his first tour on a naval supply ship. Nine months later their first child was born. She and the baby lived on the base. They moved around a lot, and it seemed as though each time they moved they had another child.

At 25 she had four children and found that the cost of raising them was getting expensive. She and a friend traded off daycare, and she took a part-time job as a nurse's aide at the base hospital. With her husband gone so much, she was tired but really liked her work and hoped to be able to go to school to get her license.

Her marriage vow eventually succumbed to the pressures of military life. Her next marriage couldn't stand the pressures of a blended family with seven children. By her third marriage, her kids were beginning to leave the house, and she was finding more time to develop her career.

She finally got the education she had wanted. She began working full-time as an L.P.N. After she built up her experience, she transferred to a private hospital that also paid tuition reimbursement. She returned to college to get her Bachelor's and eventually received her R.N.

Susan had not only accumulated a lot of addresses, a lot of children and stepchildren, and a lot of ex-husbands, she had also accumulated a lot of retirement benefits in different systems. The time on the military bases qualified her for federal retirement benefits. Her time at the state hospital qualified her for her state's public retirement system. The 20 years at the private hospital brought her more than enough credits in the Social Security system to receive a check from them as well. She had also tried to contribute a little into the voluntary retirement plans of each employer for whom she had worked. She also had been married to her second husband for more than 10 years and qualified to receive half of his Social Security if she hadn't remarried.

Her current husband has a similar patchwork quilt of retirement plans, and they just scratch their heads when they think about them. They are both 62 and know that the gong will sound soon, and they will have no choice but to figure it out. They both like their work, and they don't feel they can afford to retire early. But they hope that retirement is in their near future. They both received their reports from the Social Security office this year and tossed them in a pile of things to do later. They have decided that it may be time to open them up and see what they say.

Chapter 7

Performance Evaluation

It's time to review the performance of your main sources of retirement income: Social Security (or public pension), corporate pension and personal savings. Let's take a quick look at each before we make any course corrections.

Did Social Security Do Its Job?

Have you ever noticed how our lawmakers in Washington find ways to make our lives difficult, but don't apply the same rules to themselves? One of the most powerful laws passed by Congress in the last 25 years is ERISA, which told employers how they have to manage pension funds that they collect from your paycheck or that they contribute on your behalf into a pension fund. This law has helped to create one of the most secure private retirement pension systems in the world. Actuaries, accountants, attorneys, and pension-fund administrators get paid a lot of money to make sure that these funds follow the law.

But Congress has not passed a similar law requiring the Social Security Administration to do the same thing. The Social Security system is an "in and out" system. You pay in, they send it out. It reminds you of your teenagers' allowances, doesn't it? When you retire someday, you will hope that someone is paying in so that you can get your money out, because the money you paid in is long gone.

Estimated average monthly Social Security benefits:

All Retired Workers	$845
Aged Couple, Both Receiving Benefits	$1,410
Widowed Mother and Two Children	$1,696
Aged Widow(er) Alone	$811

Now, there are some years when the fund has a surplus and that's been cause for a lot of argument recently. Some people refer to the surplus as money sitting there waiting for you to retire. Others know that the surplus has been invested in the Federal Government securities and the Government has spent it on the current costs of operations. Now, technically, their books say that they owe this money back to the Social Security Trust Fund and they'll pay it back someday, but when they do it will come out of your income taxes. There's that word Trust again—interesting use of it. If an investment company did this, their managers would have been arrested and jailed years ago.

But, the voters (that's you) continue to elect representatives who work with the numbers so that the system continues and I believe that it will continue to function for some time. When you get ready to retire, Social Security will be there in some form and your benefit will be calculated based on some formula. It's interesting to note that the Social Security Administration has a different formula for calculating benefits depending upon what year you were born and, so far, they only have formulas up through 1938. So, if you were born in 1939 or later, you don't know what your formula is.

Let me explain the 1938 formula because future formulas will probably have some resemblance to this, or at least the underlying principles may be the same. The first thing they do is take your earnings in each year that you worked and they multiply it by an index factor that translates the number into today's dollars. So, for instance, if you worked in 1970 and made $5,000, you would multiply that by a factor of 4.67 (see the following table) resulting in the equivalent of $23,350, in today's dollars. But if you earned $8,000 in 1971, you would only be able to count $7,800, the maximum for that year. You then take your earnings (up to the maximum) from each year that you worked and you multiply them by these factors.

Social Security Conversion Factors

Year	Your Earnings	Up To 2000 Dollars	×	Inflation Factor	=
1951	_____	3600	×	10.31	= _____
1952	_____	3600	×	9.71	= _____
1953	_____	3600	×	9.19	= _____
1954	_____	3600	×	9.15	= _____
1955	_____	4200	×	8.74	= _____
1956	_____	4200	×	8.17	= _____
1957	_____	4200	×	7.93	= _____
1958	_____	4200	×	7.86	= _____
1959	_____	4800	×	7.49	= _____
1960	_____	4800	×	7.2	= _____
1961	_____	4800	×	7.06	= _____
1962	_____	4800	×	6.73	= _____
1963	_____	4800	×	6.56	= _____
1964	_____	4800	×	6.31	= _____
1965	_____	4800	×	6.2	= _____
1966	_____	6600	×	5.84	= _____
1967	_____	6600	×	5.54	= _____
1968	_____	7800	×	5.18	= _____
1969	_____	7800	×	4.9	= _____

continues

Social Security Conversion Factors (continued)

Year	Your Earnings	Up To 2000 Dollars	×	Inflation Factor	=	
1970	_____	7800	×	4.67	=	_____
1971	_____	7800	×	4.44	=	_____
1972	_____	9000	×	4.05	=	_____
1973	_____	10800	×	3.81	=	_____
1974	_____	13200	×	3.59	=	_____
1975	_____	14100	×	3.34	=	_____
1976	_____	15300	×	3.13	=	_____
1977	_____	16500	×	2.95	=	_____
1978	_____	17700	×	2.73	=	_____
1979	_____	23900	×	2.51	=	_____
1980	_____	25900	×	2.31	=	_____
1981	_____	29700	×	2.1	=	_____
1982	_____	32400	×	1.99	=	_____
1983	_____	35700	×	1.89	=	_____
1984	_____	37800	×	1.79	=	_____
1985	_____	39600	×	1.72	=	_____
1986	_____	42000	×	1.67	=	_____
1987	_____	43800	×	1.57	=	_____
1988	_____	45000	×	1.49	=	_____
1989	_____	48000	×	1.44	=	_____
1990	_____	51300	×	1.37	=	_____
1991	_____	53400	×	1.32	=	_____
1992	_____	55500	×	1.26	=	_____
1993	_____	57600	×	1.25	=	_____
1994	_____	60600	×	1.22	=	_____
1995	_____	61200	×	1.17	=	_____
1996	_____	62700	×	1.11	=	_____
1997	_____	65400	×	1.05	=	_____

Year	Your Earnings	Up To 2000 Dollars	×	Inflation Factor	=	
1998	_____	68400	×	1	=	_____
1999	_____	72600	×	1	=	_____
2000	_____	75000	×	1	=	_____
2000	_____	76200	×	1	=	_____
2001	_____	80400	×	1	=	_____

Then you take the top 35 answers, add them up, and divide them by 35 to get your average indexed yearly earnings. Then, divide that by 12 to get your average monthly earnings. What you're looking at is your average monthly income if there had been no inflation and all the dollars that you made in your life were 2000 dollars.

Then you calculate your monthly benefit from Social Security.

1. 90 percent of the first $531 (which equals $447)
2. 32 percent of the next $2,681 (which equals $858)
3. 15 percent of any amount over that
4. Total of 1. 2. and 3.

Add these three results. This will give you your monthly benefit. Let's compare this to a private savings program. If you had put your contribution to Social Security into a private investment over that 35 years and you began drawing it out at retirement you would see the following results:

❖ At 3 percent on your money, after inflation and taxes, you would run out of money in eight years.

❖ At 5 percent, after inflation and taxes, you would run out of money in ten years.

❖ At 7 percent, after inflation and taxes, you would run out of money in thirteen years.

Beginning at age 65, 13 years would only take you to age 78 and we know that our life expectancy is longer than that. What is paying the difference is your employer's contribution. So, what it looks like to me is that you may get a fairly decent interest rate on the monies you've paid into Social Security, especially since there is a lifetime guarantee on these benefits. You cannot outlive your Social Security benefits.

Granddaughter's Taxes

The only problem is that it is not your money that is coming back to you—it is money from your granddaughter's contributions. Raise her well.

This should also give us some clue as to why the system may be in trouble. If this money had been invested in a private sector pension fund, the law would have required those fund managers to make very conservative assumptions and therefore, your benefit would probably not be as much. You would not be able to rely on the money of the other people paying into the fund to pay out your benefits, except in the case where people who leave the company or die early are forfeiting part of their money.

Elderly Women Living in Poverty

Without Social Security, more than half of elderly women would be living in poverty. However, even with Social Security, older women are nearly twice as likely as older men to be poor.

—*Older Women's League*

So, the answer to the question of whether Social Security did its job or not, has two parts. The first is, has Congress continued to allow the fund to function using the monies from current workers so that your benefits are technically higher than they would be if you were operating only on the money that you had paid in? My advice would be to vote early and often.

The second part of the answer lies in whether or not they know who you are, they know where you've worked, and they know what you've made. This is something that you learn with what is now called a Social Security Statement, formerly known as Personal Earnings and Benefits Statement. This is the form that they mail to you once a year, a couple of months before your birthday. If you haven't gotten one yet, it's because you either moved or you were being audited at the time the Social Security office asked the IRS for your address. To correct this, you can order your own Social Security statement and make sure that the IRS has your correct address so that the next time your number comes up the proper address will be forwarded to the Social Security Administration.

Accurate Social Security Statements

One thing to note about the Social Security statements is that they will make an assumption for you about your future earnings and it may not be what you are planning to earn. You can sign onto their web site www.ssa.gov or call in a request for a statement 1-800-772-1213 that has the assumptions that you know to be accurate.

When you project your future earnings, do not include adjustments for inflation. As all of the calculations we have done in this book, the Social Security office follows the same protocol. They will give you your benefits in today's dollars. At the time you actually receive them you will be receiving cost of living adjustments (COLA). If you haven't worked enough to accumulate 40 credits, the report will tell you how many credits you have. A credit used to be a quarter of employment, so if you've worked 10 years or more, you're solid. A credit is now $830 of earnings in a year. So, if you have earned $3,320 this year, you have earned four credits. You don't need to earn that over the four quarters of the year. You could earn it in one day if you're lucky enough to demand that pay rate.

You can also give them different retirement dates and allow them to calculate your benefits for you. Since you know how to calculate your own benefits now, you can do it yourself or you can ask them for help. The formula that I gave you just now was assuming a normal retirement age, which is based on your birth date and ranges from 65 to 68. If you choose to retire early (62 to 66), your benefits will be reduced by 20 to 30 percent for your entire retirement. Once again, you can use your knowledge of present value to see if it makes sense for you to wait to claim your benefits.

You're also entitled to half of your husband's Social Security benefits if you're currently married, if they are more than yours. You don't get both. If you're divorced from someone who you were married to for 10 years or more, you're entitled to half his benefits. The difference is, if you're currently married you have to wait until your husband retires to claim your benefits. If you're not currently married, and you've been divorced for two years, you can claim your ex-husband's benefits at your normal retirement age. The problem is, if you're divorced, it's tricky to get that information from the Social Security Administration before your husband retires. He can request it, but you may have trouble convincing them that you have a right to see it.

Did Your Employer Do Their Job?

You worked all those years and you thought you were working for your employer. Well, they had a job, too, and it was your job to supervise them and make sure they did it right. Each year, when they send you a W-2 Form, they are also required to send the Social Security Administration a reporting of your wages and your contributions to the fund. If they didn't do that, or if they had your Social Security number wrong, then your earnings from that year will not be showing on your Social Security statement.

This is only critical if those earnings help you to exceed your 40 credit requirement or if they were during one of your high earning years. Many times the wages from early in your working life, even after adjusted for inflation, do not come out to be in the top 35. But, this is why it's important to keep up with those statements and make sure that Social Security has the numbers right. Most people are taught that you only need to keep tax returns for five to seven years and that's true with regards to your obligation to pay income taxes. But, your need for accurate earnings' records extends until you actually begin claiming your Social Security benefits.

Once you see an accurate reporting on your Benefit's Statement and you have a copy of that statement, you're probably not going to need supporting documents to verify that in the future. But, if it's not on there, you may be asked to prove your earnings for that year. If your employer is still in business, they may be able to explain to you what happened and why that information isn't reflected in your Social Security file. Chances are that the employers that didn't report accurately are also no longer in business, so you'll need to show income records from some other source. You may be able to order a copy of your tax return from that year from the IRS. Obviously, a W-2 or a pay stub would be wonderful evidence. Beyond that, anything that proved you worked there and showed your income amount would be a good start.

Corrections to Social Security Statements

If you have a problem with your statement, you should first contact your local office or call 1-800-772-1213. If you still need additional help you may write to:

Social Security Administration
Office of Public Inquiries
6401 Security Blvd.
Room 4-C-5 Annex
Baltimore, MD 21235-6401

The other equally important job that your employer had to do for you was to manage the pension fund that they and you were contributing to. From taking your contribution out of your paycheck to actually giving you a benefit check someday, there are a million and one steps, requirements, forms, and processes to follow. There are huge penalties and grave consequences if your employer doesn't follow these rules. So, while you do not have to show up at your benefits department door each year and ask to see the paperwork, it doesn't mean that they can't make administrative mistakes or minor errors in judgment that will affect your retirement check.

Women's Pensions

Women need richer retirement accounts because of their work patterns. The median pension for women is half that for men. And two of three women are in jobs that don't provide retirement benefits either through a 401(k) savings plan or a traditional pension.

—*U.S. Labor Department*

For defined benefits plans most employers will be able to provide you with a statement of estimated benefits, just as the Social Security office has done. Once again these benefits should be stated in today's dollars and allow you to see the purchasing power of that benefit. If your retirement date is several years out, you should expect to see those numbers adjusted for inflation when you actually retire and each year after that if your benefit includes a cost-of-living adjustment. It is also important to learn if those adjustments will be compounded each year—or calculated against your original benefit. This can make a big difference if you live a long time.

Did You Do Your Job?

I know, it's *all* your job. We've been through that already. No one is going to take responsibility for your life, without making you miserable in the process. Even the pieces managed by the government, your partner, your employer and your pension administrators were still your job. The day you decided that you would just stand by and trust them to make decisions that would ensure you a great retirement is the day that your retirement plan came crashing down. Claiming you didn't know how things were going to turn out doesn't put food on the table when you're eighty-five. It just doesn't.

Your main job has been to manage your income and expenses so that you have been funding your additional retirement funds to the level you will need when you reach High Retirement. Your secondary assignment has been to make good investment decisions with the money that you have assigned to this job. If you have learned to accept the risk you like and avoid the risks you don't, then you are probably happy with the size of your retirement fund right now. As you near retirement you will be making slightly different investment choices that we'll cover in the next chapter.

Women Are Conservative Investors

Even when women do save for retirement, they tend to save less and invest more conservatively than men. As a result, single women are on track to have a smaller retirement income than single men and couples.

—*The WEFA Group for Oppenheimer Management*

Now we have to have another one of those heart-to-heart talks. Onto Trojans—the horse, that is. There is a Trojan Horse in the 401(k) industry. It comes riding in looking like it's going to save the day, and ends up ruining your financial security. Most of the plan administrators in the country are still polishing up their saddles, not truly understanding how devastating this scoundrel is. One Fortune 500 employer with 50,000 participants in their 401(k) plan has half of their employees riding this horse every year.

Have you figured it out yet? This horse is a 401(k) loan. The IRS rules allow the plan designers to either allow you to make what are called hardship withdrawals or loans. Most newer plans have opted for the loans. There are some limits, which they must follow. For example, you may only borrow up to half of your account or $50,000, whichever is less.

I will admit that there are some specific situations where it might make financial sense to take a loan from your 401(k) plan but I'm not going to tell you what they are. There are other equally rational solutions for those needs that you should use instead. I have heard all the arguments: you're paying interest to yourself; it's your money to begin with; the interest is lower than the credit union; yada yada yada. Let me make this as simple as I can—don't do it.

If your head was spinning during the present value chapter, I can't even imagine how dizzy you'll get trying to measure the impact that this action will have on your retirement plan. The cost is high, the risks are many and the decision is faulty.

Now, let me tell you how I *really* feel. If you have been encouraged to participate in a pre-tax 401(k) before you have accumulated three months of your income in a *non*-tax-deferred savings account, you have been duped. You must begin your journey toward financial security with an emergency fund that you can get to if you need it, when you need it, without paying interest, without paying a penalty and without incurring taxes.

This emergency fund is the beginning of your retirement savings and will be there if you are lucky enough to not have any emergencies along the way. When you place money in a tax-deferred investment you are creating *capital*. Remember the money that goes to work for you when you don't anymore? Some 401(k) savings plans have an after-tax option. Withdrawals are allowed, but may be limited to a few a year. This is a wonderful place to put a true emergency fund. You will not be tempted to use it for a weekend getaway, but it will serve you well in an emergency. As soon as you build up the three months, you can check the box that says pre-tax and you're off and running.

Thousands of workers are walking into their benefits departments each day and asking for these loans. The administration of 401(k) loans has become a full-time job for clerks all across the country. If you are borrowing this money for a car, a refrigerator, a furnace, a divorce, or a vacation, you have not fully balanced your budget. Your short-term savings, in a statement savings account at your bank or credit union, is where you need to go for these needs, not your long-term retirement savings. Building up short-term savings is the most difficult financial planning task you need to tackle to be able to truly guarantee your future retirement security.

Remember the annoying public service announcements, "It's eleven o'clock. Do you know where your kids are?" Well, I feel like we know each other well enough at this point for me to ask you, "It's the eleventh hour, do you know how you're going to retire?" If the answer is "Yes, sort of," then the next chapter will give you some catch-up strategies. But if you are really feeling like hiding in a hole right now, it's time to go back to the beginning of the book and work on your plan, seriously this time. Waiting will only make it worse. Now is the time.

The Bottom Line

Ask questions and gather information now. Waiting until you are at retirement age is too late to make any adjustments. Even good employees have performance reviews on a regular basis. Your plan should, too.

Daddy, can I have a dollar?" Elsie can remember it like it was yesterday. Sometimes it's easier to remember than yesterday. His answer was always the same: "Don't spend it all in one place."

Every Saturday morning she would run with her big brothers to the five-and-dime on the square to buy a pickle. She always liked the ones with more bumps—they were good luck. She liked the way the change sounded in her pocket on the way home. She felt rich.

Three quarters and two dimes. She would put them in her special pickle jars on her bureau. One was for her future—it got two quarters because her future was a long time. Another was for the pony she was going to buy. It got a quarter because they were expensive and her mom said they eat a lot. One dime for candy after school and the other for church tomorrow. She knew God liked dimes the best.

Elsie found boys before she could afford that pony. The money came in handy for hair curlers and other things her mom said she didn't need. Her "future" pickle jar overflowed and her daddy took her to the bank to buy a savings bond. He was very proud of her. He told her she was learning to take care of herself and her country at the same time.

Before Elsie's dad died 20 years ago, he told her again how proud he was of her. She was his special pickle.

She was sorry he didn't live long enough to spend all his money. She didn't need it. The bonds he left her were about to mature. She called a friend to take her to the bank this morning to buy some more.

Chapter 8

Add It All Up

Your circumstances are always changing and the investment environment is changing as well. Once you put your plan into place, you are not done. Doing periodic evaluations to see where you are is critical to reaching your goals.

Are You Playing Catch-Up?

So, what does it look like now? Doing a review of your overall plan can sometimes be like trying on that suit you haven't worn in two years, it just doesn't fit quite the same as it used to. It's still the same suit, same size, same color, but you've changed just a little and now you need to decide if you're going to buy a new suit or get back on that exercise bike. But you know one thing for sure, wearing the suit is going to be really uncomfortable.

Each time you recalculate where you are and where you want to be at retirement you may find out that your previous assumptions no longer fit. There's certainly a chance that you're ahead of where you thought you would be at this point. The only danger in finding that out is a false sense of euphoria that may evaporate those gains quickly. So keep watching it each year from now until retirement and make sure that you really are ahead before you make any drastic changes in your plan.

If you're staring at the other end of the donkey, you're going to need to make some tougher decisions. If you're learning that with less than 10 years to go to your retirement date, the rate at which you're saving will not allow you the retirement income that you feel you need, then you're going to need to make some adjustments. What most people in this situation do is:

1. Worry about the problem for a while.
2. Find a way to talk themselves out of the fact that there is a problem.
3. Go ahead and retire at the age they had planned.
4. Spend their retirement years continuing to worry about whether they'll run out of money.
5. Run out of money and become dependent on family members.

So your choice is to think about it now and take some corrective action or spend your retirement worrying about it. Only you can decide which would be more comfortable for you.

If you'd like to do something about it now, let's look at the different variables that you have control of:

1. Adjust your current budget to put more in your retirement fund.
2. Adjust your retirement budget down to need less income.
3. Retire later.
4. Invest differently to increase earnings both before and after retirement.
5. Earn additional income during retirement.

In order to accomplish the first two objectives, it's helpful to go back to Chapter 3, "A Balancing Act," and analyze the budgets you have remaining. You also may find some hints in the coming chapters regarding insurance, housing, and taxes that might help you fine-tune some of your assumptions so that your budgets are more easily managed.

Retiring later may be one of those options that seem reasonable to you. This can have a very big impact on the numbers depending upon how close you are to retirement. Another solution is to retire partially, working part-time during retirement until your plan balances.

The Pieces of the Pie

Maybe you decide that your budget is just about as tight as it can be and your retirement date is also fixed and that you'd be more comfortable taking a little more risk with your investments in order to gain a higher rate of return. I'd like to teach you a system called "asset allocation" which can help you understand if your investments are in the right place and if you've done what you can to manage the risk.

Whether or not you've ever heard those big words before, you already know how to do this. I'm going to guess that you've been on a diet at least once in your life, if not right now. When we go on diets, we have some formula in our heads, or some plan, or some menu, that we hope will work this time. Some of the more recent diets have helped us to understand that we need to know the split between how much protein, carbohydrates, and fats we need each day. They recommend that we eat certain percentages of each of them (such as 45 percent protein, 35 percent carbohydrate, 20 percent fat).

That is an asset allocation. You've taken three main nutrients and determined what percentage will be the best for your situation. When you do this with your money, you have to look at everything you own and see what percentages you have in each category. Let's go back to the five things you can do with your money. Remember the five things are:

1. Keep it as money.
2. Spend it on something.
3. Buy something that you keep.

4. Loan it to someone.

5. Gamble it.

When we think of assets, all of these except number two become relevant. So, I'd like you to think about everything you own and make a list on the following chart and check the box next to it:

1. Are you keeping this asset as money? (Meaning is it in a CD, savings account, or money market account?)

2. Is this something that you've bought to keep? (Like a stock, house, or some other investment.)

3. Have you loaned it to someone? (Either a personal loan or a bond to a government or corporation.)

4. Are you gambling it? (Is it in a place that is not really an investment?)

Put the value of that asset in the column relating to which type of asset it is. Then total each of the four columns. To determine whether your mutual funds are in bonds, which would go in the loan column, or they're stocks, which would go in the buy something you keep column, you may need to call the fund company or use a mutual fund tracking company Web site, like Morningstar.com.

Asset Allocation Analysis

Asset	Cash?	Something to Keep?	Loan to Someone?	Gamble?
_____	_____	_____	_____	_____
_____	_____	_____	_____	_____
_____	_____	_____	_____	_____
_____	_____	_____	_____	_____
_____	_____	_____	_____	_____
_____	_____	_____	_____	_____
_____	_____	_____	_____	_____
Totals	_____	_____	_____	_____

Now look at the totals in each column. Your cash column should hold between three and six months of income. The gambling column should be a very small percentage, if any, of your total assets, and the rest will be between the other two columns. At this point in your retirement plan, you're still looking at very long-term needs for this money. Having more money in stocks than bonds would allow you a higher long-term return. This may be where you find the additional money you need to balance your plan. Having money in bonds will give you a flatter return, usually a little lower than stocks in the long run.

Think about how comfortable you would be taking more risk to earn more return. Balance that against your comfort with making the other changes that would balance your plan. If you're very comfortable with your portfolio the way it is right now, you may need to get comfortable with the notion that you're going to retire a little later or put more into your fund between now and when you're going to retire.

There is no magic formula, just like there is no magic diet, for what percentages should be in these different assets at different points in your life. All of the advisors that you seek help from will have different opinions and you need to listen to those opinions and see if it makes sense for you in your current situation.

Match Goals with Returns

If, for instance, you are overfunded right now and very comfortable, putting more in bond funds will give you more security and, possibly, more peace of mind since you can do without the higher returns. So work with percentages that you are comfortable with and track your investments to make sure you're meeting those goals.

Types of Investment Risk

There are so many types of risks in the investments that you might choose that it's pretty depressing to name them all. But a short discussion might help you start thinking about the types of risks that you would be comfortable taking and the ones you wouldn't.

First, there are systematic risks. These are the ones that would happen to all investments of a particular type.

❖ Market risk: Caused by the reaction of investors to political, social, or economic events. They just decide they don't like your type of investment as much anymore and won't pay as much for it.

❖ Interest rate risk: What happens to the prices of bonds when interest rates go up and down.

❖ Reinvestment risk: The chance you take that when one investment matures, you will be able to find another investment earning the same rate.

❖ Purchasing power risk: The risk that inflation will erode the value of your investment at its maturity.

❖ Liquidity risk: The uncertainty that goes along with your ability to turn the investment into cash in a relatively short period of time.

The other type are, you guessed it, unsystematic risks. These factors are dependent on features that are specific to that investment. This is the type of risk that can be reduced by what is called *diversification*—buying different types of investments.

❖ Business risk: Defines the uncertainty of the investment to maintain its payments on your investment or its growth that adds to your rate of return.

❖ Default risk: Similar to business risk but is usually applied to government securities.

❖ Financial risk: Related to how much debt has been used to finance the firm or property.

Any amount of risk that you choose to assume on top of the risk-free rate should bring you a higher return. When an investment salesperson offers you a prospectus or a historical view of a particular investment that shows a rate higher than your risk-free rate, you can ask the question, "Where was the risk?" What risk did that investor have to assume in order to achieve that higher rate?

This brings us right back to the concept of trust. You know that riding with your brother-in-law to your family's cabin on the lake will get you there faster but you also know there is some risk associated with riding with your brother-in-law. So, you sit in the backseat and you take a book and you try not to pay attention. Once you've made the decision that you want to get there in three hours instead of four, you just need to trust him.

It's the same thing with your investments. You can ride with your husband, who's never had a ticket in his life and refuses to get within five miles of the speed limit. You are absolutely sure that you will not be hurt during that trip. You don't have to trust him. His previous behavior has assured you that there is no risk, but you also know that you will miss out on half the fun by getting there later.

Is this starting to sound a little bit like this retirement you're planning? Go slow. Get there safe. It'll just be a little later. Take a little risk, probably still get there, but get there when you can still have time to enjoy the afternoon sun.

Diversification

Back to that diet. Once you figure out how much protein, carbohydrates, and fat you need, you still have to figure out what food you're going to eat to get each. If you've ever tried one of those diets where you eat the same food for weeks at a time, you know it doesn't work.

It's exactly the same with your investments. If you determine that you would like to have 80 percent of your money in stocks, you can't have it all in the same stock. In fact, you probably don't even want it all in the same stock mutual fund, which is a grouping of stocks, managed by a professional manager. So, we need to do a second chart to determine how much variety you have in the stock funds that you've selected. There are two things that are important:

1. Does the fund invest in small, medium, or large companies?
2. What industries are the companies in?

Diversification Analysis

Stock/Mutual Fund	Small	Mid	Large	Sector	Foreign?
_____	_____	_____	_____	_____	_____
_____	_____	_____	_____	_____	_____
_____	_____	_____	_____	_____	_____
_____	_____	_____	_____	_____	_____
_____	_____	_____	_____	_____	_____
_____	_____	_____	_____	_____	_____
_____	_____	_____	_____	_____	_____
_____	_____	_____	_____	_____	_____
_____	_____	_____	_____	_____	_____

The terms you'll be looking for to determine its size will say something like "small cap" or "small capitalization," "mid cap," and "large cap." Industries might be something like tech stocks, medical stocks, or utility stocks. A third criteria which some people like to look at is whether you're investing in foreign or domestic stocks.

Once again, there's no magic formula, but the more variety that you can get without incurring too many management fees or too much hassle on your part is generally good. It's exactly the same as your diet. The more variety you get in the food you eat, the more you can ensure that you're getting the nutrients you need. If you have a wide variety of stock funds, what you're ensuring is that a crisis in one sector of the economy will not ruin your entire retirement.

Where I see this as a problem is when companies encourage their employees to purchase stock in their employer. Many employees feel a sense of loyalty and pride in owning stock in their own employer. Many times they get to purchase the stock at a below-market rate and many times their employers match their purchase with additional shares. This is a wonderful way to accumulate capital toward retirement.

But, the closer you get to retirement, the more important it is to begin to diversify that stock into other holdings. You're taking a big risk that its value will be low when you retire. Go back to your percentages and determine what percentage of your stock holdings you feel comfortable having in your company's stock and make sure that it hasn't exceeded that amount.

Windfall Additions to Your Retirement Plan

Divorce Settlements

If you have, or are almost, divorced from a husband who has accumulated money in a deferred pension plan, in most situations half of that asset is yours. You certainly may negotiate some other asset in exchange for it, but receiving retirement fund monies takes a little bit of management and will add to your calculations for funds that you will have available at your retirement. Some companies, especially those with defined benefit plans, may hold onto your portion of the money and when your husband retires, you would get a portion of that check.

The more common scenario now, though, is that a distribution is made from the plan to you. This is referred to as a "Qualified Domestic Relations Order" (QDRO for short). The money comes out of the plan with no early withdrawal penalty and you would have to immediately "roll it over" into an IRA in order to avoid taxes. Normally, this money cannot be deposited into your employer's plan. So if you're doing your retirement plan both ways, with and without him, this is the way to calculate how much you would have if you became divorced. Remember that, likewise, he has rights to half of your funds. So, it depends upon who has accumulated more as to which direction the distribution would go.

Changing Employers

Each time you leave an employer, any monies in a defined contribution plan, and any vested amounts in a defined benefit plan, become yours. If the amount is under $5,000, they will require you to take it with you. What you do is deposit it in an IRA, which avoids penalties and postpones taxes. You can also leave monies on account in certain plans. The public pension plans are the prime example, but many private pension funds will also hold onto your benefits and allow you to take payments at retirement. If you're building your retirement fund in a 401(k) but have other IRAs that you've accumulated, make sure when you do your asset allocation analysis, you include them all.

Inheritances

Sometimes, prior to retirement, a family member will die and leave you investments that could be applied to your retirement fund. When assets are passed from their estate, the basis in these assets is immediately "stepped up." What this means is, that if your mother bought a share of Microsoft stock for $5 and it's worth $100 when she dies, there would be a capital gain of $95. But you don't have to pay tax on that capital gain because her death caused the basis to go up to $100. So, when you inherit stocks and other assets you can immediately trade them and not pay capital gain tax on them, so you can place them into your asset allocation preferences to meet your needs. Just like her clothes may not fit you, her investment choices may not, either.

If the money she left you was still in a tax-deferred pension plan or IRA at her death, there will be rules about how you can continue to defer the taxes. You can always pay the tax right away and take them out of their tax-deferred status, but you do have some options to defer that tax and allow the money to continue to grow without being taxed. The rules are complicated, however, and this would be a situation when hiring a CPA or CFP to explain them to you would be well worth it.

When you are transferring assets from one investment to another, a system known as dollar-cost averaging is one that works for many investors. Very simply, it means making a purchase of shares in that stock or stock fund for the same dollar amount on the same day each month. It allows you to average out the highs and lows in the stock so you do not have to be Carnack the Magnificent to determine the exact date that is the best to buy it. The same logic applies when you are selling an investment, like one you inherit. Many financial institutions will set this up for you automatically.

The Bottom Line

Make sure to take all your assets into account when you do your periodic evaluation. If you've got too much fat in your diet, it doesn't matter how great the protein is. Keep everything allocated according to a formula you are comfortable with and keep it diversified.

Kathy never liked paying her bills, least of all her insurance premiums. She always saw them as a necessary evil. Because her life had been relatively trauma free, she had the good fortune of being able to complain that she hadn't used much of the benefits available in her insurance policies.

She had what she believed to be the normal coverage at her employer. But, to be honest, she never really thought about it much. Her life had been filled with raising children, her job, her home and recently, the birth of her grandchildren. She didn't spend much time thinking about what could go wrong.

As she had gotten older she had noticed that more and more offers were coming in the mail for insurance products that she really felt she was too young to worry about. She was sure they had gotten her name from a mailing list and they really weren't marketing to her.

Her car insurance agent of many years had retired a couple of years back and a new guy had taken over his office. She had only met him once when she stopped by the office to drop off the paperwork on her new car. One day she got a letter from him encouraging her to call for an appointment for an insurance check-up. "Check-up," she thought, "what do I need a check-up for? Things have been going pretty well up to now and I just can't stand talking about all that insurance stuff. He'll just want to sell me more insurance I'll never claim on."

Then she thought about the life insurance policy she and her husband had taken out when the kids were little and she wondered if she really needed that much insurance anymore. Maybe she would stop by and talk to him about dropping it. But, that's the last thing he wanted to hear and he'd probably talk her into buying something else with the money she was saving from the life insurance.

Chapter 9

Insurance Adjustments

Insurance is one of those things we all hate to have to deal with. Prior to retirement there are several key decisions to make and new information to learn. As annoying as it is, not knowing can cost you.

Long-Term-Care Insurance

Remember old folks' homes? When I was growing up in Sidney, Ohio, everybody used to talk about going out to live at the "home" when they got older. I always thought this was a pretty neat thing because my grandpa had helped to start the home. The way it looked to me, people sort of went there to sit until they died. They took really good care of them there and heck, all their friends were there.

Well, we don't call them "homes" anymore. They're called "retirement villages," "senior cities," or "care facilities" and, gosh, are they expensive. About the cheapest you can find is around $3,000 a month and they go way up from there. I don't know many people that can afford that much money for room and board while they're working let alone after they retire. So when many people express the fear of outliving their money, it's this sort of expense that comes to mind.

When your money runs out, the Medicaid Program begins to pick up the tab. Lots of careful strategies have been developed to make sure that this happens sooner than later. But, as one retiree explained to me, "I didn't work this hard all my life to be able to prove to the government that I'm a pauper."

A few years ago, the insurance industry designed a type of policy that allows you an option to hold onto your assets and still have quality care that you may need during your Low Retirement. The appearance of long-term care insurance was a response by the insurance industry to the financial reality that living longer may mean living longer in need of nursing home or home health-care services.

This type of insurance is still only offered by a handful of companies but most insurance agencies will carry one or more of those policies. *A.M. Best* rates the companies as to financial stability and your insurance commissioner may have a comparison of features of the policies available in your state. You can't buy long-term health insurance until you're 30, with some companies, and generally after 50. You cannot purchase this type of policy if you are already disabled.

There is some chance that you won't end up in a nursing home, certainly there are people who die instantly and never experience a disability before death. But, there are others who spend their Low Retirement years in the care of family members. But, remember that in your plan you are assuming that you will have "X" number of years spent in your Low Retirement period. So your job as the planner is to determine whether or not this type of insurance allows you the options that you would want to have during that time period.

Here's how it works. You will be charged a premium based on the
age you are when you purchase the policy. That premium, with
most policies, will remain level for the duration of your life.
Premiums can ordinarily only be raised for an entire class of poli-
cyholder. Your insurance commissioner should have information
on which companies have previously raised their rates.

Your premiums will vary wildly depending upon the benefits that
you choose. First, you will decide how much money you would
like to be paid per day if you are in a nursing home. A couple of
calls to nursing homes of your choice will give you an idea what
the current rates are and that's a real good place to start.

Next, you will choose a waiting period. This is the number of
days or weeks that you would be in the nursing home before
your policy would kick in. You would be responsible for paying
the cost of those days yourself.

Then, you'll choose a benefit period, which is the amount of
time that the policy will pay for you to be in the nursing home.
You might be interested to know that the average stay in a nursing home is 24 months, but over half the stays are less than six
months. There is more effort being put into rehabilitative treatments allowing you to return home than in past years.

Another decision you will need to make is whether you choose
an inflation rider on your policy. Rather than trying to guess
what nursing homes will cost in the year that your plan says you
will need care, you can instead purchase a benefit that would
take care of you in today's dollars. The rider would automatically
add benefits to your policy up until you use the policy and then
continue through your benefit period. If you don't choose the

inflation rider you either need to start with a much higher benefit level, or know that you will be subsidizing your benefit with
personal money at the time you need the service.

One of the most important features of these policies is the Home
Health Care Benefit. I haven't met anyone who wouldn't rather
be at home during a period of disability if there were any way to
do it. These policies allow a reduced benefit, many times half of
the stated nursing home benefits, to allow for home health care
workers to care for you in your home. This is one of the bigger
differences between the options you have under a private policy
and the options you have under Medicaid. This is a feature that
will be an option for you and will add cost to your premium.
Some clients I have worked with purchase these policies solely so
that they have that option; others determine that the cost is not
worth the added benefit.

Life Insurance

Kathy was on the right track when she thought that she might
need to adjust her level of life insurance. She was thinking that
her children would not need as much cash if she were to die now
than if she had died when they were little. Her children had what
we call an insurable interest in her when they were young and
they may no longer have that same interest.

To determine if someone has an insurable interest in you, ask
yourself this question: "If I die, will someone suffer financially
from my demise; or if I continue to live, will someone benefit
financially from my continued existence?" If the answer is yes,
then that person has an insurable interest in you. This is a test
given by the insurance industry to determine whether or not
someone is allowed to own a life insurance policy on your life
and whether the death benefit might be taxable. But, this is also
a helpful tool for you to determine your life insurance needs at
any point during your life.

If you answered yes to one of the two questions, make a list of
who those folks are and think about what their financial suffering would be should you die, or what their financial benefit is as

you continue to live. It could be a one-time or short-term benefit, such as the last two college tuition payments that you might make for your son, or it could be a very long-term benefit, such as the housing and support that you provide for a disabled adult child. Think about the replacement cost of your support and services. This will give you a good idea of how much life insurance you need.

You also need to prepare for your final expenses, which can run anywhere from $5,000 to $25,000 dollars, and this can be paid for from life insurance as well. Since life insurance proceeds do not go through the probate process, many times this cash is more accessible sooner after a death than other investments.

There are, of course, other reasons to purchase life insurance. Most of them involve more complicated financial planning goals. One might desire to leave a bequest to a charity of your choosing. Another might be to have enough cash in your estate to allow one child to keep a major family asset such as a home or a business, while giving the other children an equal share of your wealth.

Cost of Life Insurance

Review all the life insurance policies that you bought four or more years ago. The cost of life insurance has dropped dramatically and you may be able to find substantial savings.

If you've determined that you would like to continue owning a life insurance contract, then the next decision would be what kind of contract. If you have reached a point where your health is no longer able to qualify you for a new contract, you'll need to read your existing contracts far enough to determine whether you have any options for changing their provisions.

Many times a term policy can be converted to a whole life policy. This would be beneficial to lock in a premium that would not increase beyond affordable in your later years, but would allow a death benefit that would be there on the day you die. This type of policy is best for purposes that are going to continue, such as caring for a disabled child or leaving money to a charity.

Your term insurance would be good to keep if your purpose for the insurance is also going to end in a specific term. With most insurance policies you can reduce the death benefit without changing policies and qualifying for new underwriting criteria. You also may be able to convert group insurance you've carried through your employer to an individual policy. Make sure you compare these rates to a policy you might start new as the insurance industry knows that people who convert life insurance are possibly in worse health than the average worker, so the rates build this in.

Life Insurance Cancellation

Never cancel an existing policy until you know you can obtain a new policy elsewhere.

Another thing that's very important to do at this point in your planning is to reexamine your beneficiary designations. If you're like most people, when you signed up for the policy years ago you wrote down your spouse or your parents as primary beneficiary and then children or siblings as your secondary beneficiary. As you age, you may decide that there would be a better distribution for that life insurance benefit. You can split a beneficiary designation any way that you want.

Disability Insurance

You know those annoying phone calls that always come at dinnertime? Think back. How many times has somebody called your home attempting to sell you disability insurance? My guess is, never. It just doesn't happen.

Disability insurance is the most undersold and underutilized insurance contract in this country, in my opinion. It has grown more important to most families than their life insurance.

Medical science has found wonderful ways to keep us alive, but not necessarily working, longer. This has increased our need for this type of insurance, but it continues to be a high source of fraud for the insurance companies to deal with. From a risk management perspective, they don't usually go out seeking customers for this type of contract.

Life Insurance Purchased

Life insurance is the most purchased and most owned of all insurance products.

—*Women Insurance Needs Study*

Most of the disability insurance is sold as groups to employers and then you are offered that policy as an individual option in a cafeteria plan or as a standard benefit available to all employees. When I ask clients what their benefits are, they normally have very little idea and haven't grasped the importance of understanding just exactly what they've got.

At this point in your planning process, you will need to revisit your disability benefits and determine if you have some options that might allow you to either save some money or structure your benefits in a more helpful way. If you've been working many years on building a good retirement fund and you are forced out of the workplace by disability, some of those retirement monies may become available to you. For instance, your Social Security retirement benefit becomes available after five months of permanent disability. Depending upon your age at disability, some companies may allow you to take early retirement and enjoy all the benefits that go along with being retired.

Your own personal savings may also impact your need for disability insurance at this point. You may be able to wait longer before you need a disability benefit or you may need less of a monthly payment because your savings can supplement that monthly income should you become disabled. You can always reduce your benefit in a disability policy that you own or increase your elimination period, which is the time you wait before your payments begin. If you do this, you might be able to buy a guaranteed option to purchase more later should you feel the need.

It's a good idea to go back to the cash flow plan that you completed in Chapter 3, "A Balancing Act," and create another column for a disability status. Research the amount of money that you would receive from your group benefits and individual policies and adjust the expenses to reflect your new lifestyle as a disabled person. See if the budget balances.

One thing to keep in mind is the taxation of disability benefits. The IRS requires that you either have paid tax on the money that you used to pay the premium or you pay tax on the benefits that you receive, but not both. So, for instance, if your employer paid the premium with money that was never added to your taxable income, then when you receive the benefits, that will be taxable income to you. On the other hand, if you paid the premium with money that had already been taxed, then when you receive your benefits, they will be tax-free.

Another thing to keep in mind is that many policies do what is called coordination of benefits. This is a fancy way to say you don't get all the money. Take the example of a woman who becomes disabled and receives a monthly disability check of $2,000 from her employer. Her disability continues past five months and her employer requires that she apply for Social Security Disability benefits, which she does. But it takes Social Security about a year to figure out that she's really disabled. (You can't be too careful!) Her monthly benefit will be $800 when it actually comes in, assuming she's not dead. The first check that she gets is over $9,000. This is not her money. She owes this back to her employer for the benefit that she was paid from her employer during a time period that she was also covered by Social Security. From that point forward her employer will only send her $1,200. She will get the additional $800 from Social Security.

Individual policies usually do not require this unless they are of the type called Income Replacement Policies. These policies increase your income back up to a predisabled level so if you are receiving income from any earned or unearned source, they would pay the rest to bring you back up to where you were before. These policies are cheaper because they're assuming that they won't be paying the full benefit for the entire benefit period.

Check out the definition of disability in your policy. It may be "own occupation" or "any occupation." A common policy type will pay you for a couple of years if you can't perform the duties of your own occupation. But, after that, you have to be so disabled that you can't perform any job. So if you own an individual disability policy, this is a good time to understand more about what you have, when it will pay, whether it coordinates benefits, how it defines disability and how long the benefits will continue.

Many policies are written to end at age 65, presuming that other retirement benefits, including Social Security, would start at that point. This would be a problem for you if your retirement date were after age 65. Ask your agent for a policy that ends at age 70.

Health Insurance

Time to wake up! I know insurance gets the award for Most Boring Topic in a Non-Fiction Book. But I want you to pay attention to this section. And then go read more about it. You can't know too much and you can't know it too soon.

Medicare and You

The Medicare programs are managed by the Health Care Financing Administration, which is part of the Federal Department of Health and Human Services. They have published regional editions of a reference book titled *Medicare & You*. They also have a *Guide to Health Insurance for People with Medicare*. You can order copies by calling 1-800-MEDICARE or logging on to www.medicare.gov.

When the Medicare program was started in the mid '60s, its purpose was to prevent a catastrophic illness from impoverishing an older American. That's why you would hear older women complaining that, "Medicare doesn't pay for prescriptions and it doesn't pay for mammograms, either!" It wasn't supposed to back then.

But as women went to work for companies that provided them with increasingly comprehensive medical insurance, they became used to having someone else pay their medical costs. At the same time more medical services became available to prevent, diagnose, treat, and cure many more ailments. And some of these procedures aren't cheap!

The first thing to understand is that Medicare begins when you turn 65. Congress has not raised the age of benefits as it has with Social Security—yet! So 65 is it. Certain disabled workers can claim benefits before 65. If you retire before 65, you must clearly understand what options you have for health coverage until you are 65. If your employer provides health benefits to retirees, make sure you fill out *every* piece of paper, on time, and keep copies. If your spouse is relying on these benefits (especially if they are younger than you) find out how to protect their benefits in the event that you die before they reach 65.

The second thing to understand is that Medicare begins when you turn 65. If you are already receiving Social Security benefits, you will be enrolled automatically. If not, you will need to sign up. If you are still working, your group insurance company will expect you to sign up for Part A (The Hospitalization coverage). If your employer has more than 20 employees, that group health plan will be your primary coverage and Medicare will pay second. If there are less than 20 employees, Medicare will become your primary coverage and your group health plan will pay second.

You may choose to sign up for Part B (The Doctors coverage) during a seven-month window that begins three months before you turn 65. The cost is currently $50 per month, paid quarterly or withheld from your monthly Social Security retirement or disability checks. There is a stiff penalty in the form of an increased premium, forever, if you miss the enrollment window. If you continue working past 65, you must sign up within six months of retiring to avoid the penalties.

So, as you approach retirement and transition into the Medicare system, you need to forget everything you've ever known about health insurance offered to workers in this country. This is a whole new tea party. You will probably be covered by Medicare and many of the other health insurance contracts you may obtain will relate to Medicare in some way.

Medicare Benefits and Costs

Benefit	Your Out-of-Pocket Cost
Part A (Hospitalization)	
Hospital stays	$792 for a stay of 1–60 days
	$198 per day for days 61–90
	$396 per day for days 91–150
Skilled Nursing Care Facility	$0 for 20 days
	Up to $97 per day for days 21–100
	All costs for day 101 on
Home Health Care, under certain conditions	No cost to you
Hospice Care, under certain conditions	$5 copay for prescriptions drugs
Part B	
Doctor's visits, excluding check-ups	$100 deductible per year
Outpatient tests and services	20% of approved amount
Outpatient mental health care	50% of approved amount
Lab services	$0
Home health care, if approved	$0

As people retired who were accustomed to having more coverage than what Medicare offered, the insurance industry responded with a type of policy called Medigap or Medicare Supplement (Med Sup for short). In most states, there are 10 standardized policy forms, labeled A through J. Your insurance commissioner will have a list of the companies that offer these policies in your state and the premiums they charge. Your State Health Insurance Assistance Program will be able to offer you guidance in selecting the plan that is right for you.

If you can afford the premiums, Medicare Supplements are a wonderful way to predict and level out your health care costs during your retirement. Depending upon the form you choose, you will have little or no out-of-pocket expenses for Medicare covered services. Forms H, I, and J do offer some prescription coverage as well. Many companies offer what is called a crossover benefit, which allows Medicare to electronically forward your claims to them, so you have very little paperwork to worry about.

Until 1997, these were the choices for people over 65. Then Congress passed the Balanced Budget Act of 1997. What, you ask, did that have to do with the price of mammograms? A great deal. Remember Hillary? While she was out stirring up emotions about health care in this country, the insurance companies and hospitals were lobbying Congress to give them a bigger piece of the Medicare pie. She lost, they won.

Congress created six models for new ways to access Medicare benefits called Medicare+Choice Options. Various hospitals, insurance companies and health maintenance organizations have developed products that follow one of these six models. You have seen the advertisements in your area and wondered what's going on, I'm sure. The Health Care Financing Administration can send you Publication HCFA-10050 that will show you the options in your area.

At first I thought these were new Medigap policies, but they are very different. They may be an HMO (Health Maintenance Organization), a PPO (Preferred Provider Organization), a PSO

(Provider Sponsored Organization), or a PFFS (Private Fee-for-Service) plan. To be enrolled in these plans, you would have to be enrolled in both Part A & B (and pay the premium) and then also pay any premium charged by the Medicare+Choice Option provider. In many cases, they are cheaper than the Medigap policies and reduce the paperwork. The managed care plans (HMO, PPO, PSO) have some of the same drawbacks that employer-purchased managed care plans have. For instance, you would have to visit one of their approved doctors and obtain a referral to a specialist.

So I am begging you to order all the publications you can find, and read them for your area. Do this well before you need to make a decision. You don't want to miss an open enrollment period or be penalized for waiting to enroll. Some things can wait until you're ready. This one can't.

Property and Casualty Insurance

As your net worth increases throughout your working life, you can afford to absorb more risks yourself. The deductibles on your car and home insurance are good examples of this. When you were just starting out, $100 was hard to come up with to fix a cracked windshield. But, now $500 or even $1,000 may be affordable for the rare occurrences when you actually file a claim. If you think back over your life and count up the number of times you had to pay a deductible on your car or homeowner's policies, it may not be that many. Ask your insurance agent what your savings might be to raise your deductible, and then add that money to your own personal savings, you will have it in the event you need to pay a deductible. In the fortunate event that you don't have any claims, then the money is yours to keep.

On the other side of the coin, however, as your net worth increases, you have the potential for larger losses in the event of a liability claim. So you would be better off to put your insurance dollars at the other end of your policies. Raising your liability limits, possibly with an umbrella policy, which raises your limits on both your car and homeowner's insurance, is a cost-effective way to do this. By this time, you probably have a good relationship established with your car and homeowner's insurance agents. They should be able to advise you professionally on what is in your best interest. But, don't forget that you're the customer and if you have questions that aren't being answered, make sure to ask them somewhere else. Be a good shopper and make sure your needs are met.

The Bottom Line

As much as you have been glued to this chapter, I would suggest that you make these decisions quickly, document your decisions well and move on with your planning. It is really a danger that you will get so interested in reading your insurance policies that it will impact your relationships. And I couldn't live with myself if that happened.

Part 3

Retirement

You made it! It's great! With all the careful planning behind us, your options are tremendous. But the reality is just sinking in. You are independent and secure, but new decisions are ahead. Investment decisions seem more important and long-term care concerns are on your mind. We'll cover the range of decisions still ahead. Everything from taxes to Social Security to investments. We'll also face the hard decisions required toward the end of our lives. It's a time for you to reflect, enjoy, and relax.

Some days were harder than others for Eva to go up and down the stairs. She and her husband put a shower in the downstairs bathroom and moved their bedroom to the first floor a couple of years ago.

But every Friday morning, like clockwork, Eva climbs the stairs, sometimes slowly, to dust the four bedrooms upstairs. The sports trophies and scouting awards are still on the shelves in the four bedrooms where her children grew up. The cribs had come back down out of the attic when the grandchildren started coming to visit, a little out of place in the rooms that still have teenager written all over them.

Their daughter-in-law and grandson lived in one for a few months while their son was stationed overseas. Eva's youngest son ends up there, predictably, in between jobs. Her daughters send their school-age kids to stay with her a couple of weeks each summer. They all have their favorite rooms to stay in. At Thanksgiving, there isn't enough room for everybody, so the kids camp out on the living room floor.

She keeps the basement rec room stocked with the latest videos, toys, and electronic gadgets, even though she isn't sure how to use most of them. The garage is still cluttered with at least six bikes, two wagons, a couple of scooters, and balls of all shapes and sizes.

Eva and her husband built the home 30 years ago, right after their youngest daughter was born. It was getting to the point where it could use a facelift. Through the cost of raising kids and getting them through college, they hadn't had a lot of extra cash to spend on redecorating. Now, it seemed like all the repairs were so expensive, and with the property taxes going up, the home seemed expensive.

They had gone out to dinner last week to celebrate their last mortgage payment. They had looked forward to this day for 30 years. They thought it would make more of a difference to them than it has. Their home, now worth $350,000, only cost $60,000 to build. The mortgage that they carried for all that time had a payment of $360. Their property taxes and insurance on the home are actually more than that today.

With rising costs of maintenance and increasing difficulty getting around to take care of it, they're wondering whether it's time to move. They can't imagine leaving behind the memories and the ability to entertain their family. The financial realities are frustrating.

Chapter 10

Housing Options

Housing needs change over time. You have two decisions: where you want to live and how you want to pay for it. Thinking about these two decisions separately allows both to become focused.

Where Do You Want to Live?

In my work with homeless families over the years I've arrived at a new definition of the word "home." That's the place where you left your clean underwear and you're pretty sure it will be there when you get back. When women and their children arrive at the family shelters around this country, many times they only have a couple of trash bags' worth of possessions with them. The tireless social workers and volunteers, who help these women begin the process of reestablishing a permanent home, start with the basics and work up from there.

Out-of-Pocket Expenditures

One of the greatest differences between preretirement and postretirement budgets is the cost of basic healthcare. In 1998, annual out-of-pocket costs ranged from 9 to 16 percent of the budgets of older Americans.

—*Older American 2000: Key Indicators of Well-Being; Federal Interagency Forum on Aging-Related Statistics*

Sometimes in retirement, due to financial or physical limitations, we begin eliminating the extras and move back toward a fairly basic lifestyle. Maintaining your evolved lifestyle requires planning to make sure that you can afford to replace things as they break. You also need the physical capacity to care for them or the money to pay someone to do it for you.

You've made housing choices much of your life. What was important to you? Was the physical house and its appearance your major concern? Was it a school district or proximity to work that made up your mind? Was it the recommendation of a friend who loved the neighborhood and the people in it? Maybe the garden had just enough sunlight or the basement had just enough storage space. Maybe the condo you bought was secure and well-maintained, or the apartment you lived in had a great landlord.

You may have purchased your first home as your "starter home," planning to acquire some equity and then move to your dream home. Your retirement housing choices can follow a similar pattern. I would suggest that you think of your housing choices as being two-stepped as well. Where do you want to live during your High Retirement and where do you want to live during your Low Retirement?

Even if your vision of retirement is sitting on the back (or front!) of a Harley, you'll probably have a home base. You may want to really develop your garden, maybe even adding a greenhouse; improve your kitchen to be able to do the gourmet cooking you've always wanted to try; or finally convert that extra bedroom into a sewing and craft studio, buying the serger you've always wanted.

Or, you may be looking to simplify things, have fewer rooms to keep clean and fewer gadgets to keep repaired. All of the financial decisions regarding your housing in retirement will spin from the answers to these questions. Where you want to live comes first. Do you have a climate you'd like to try out? Maybe mountains bring you a sense of peace. Do you want to get away from big cities and traffic and people, or are you drawn to the excitement and cultural opportunities of the major population centers.

Most Alive Places to Live

Not everyone is looking for the same thing. Here are a few of the "winners" in a recent poll:

❖ Best Small Town: Asheville, North Carolina

❖ Best College Town: Austin, Texas

❖ Best Big City: Boston, Massachusetts

❖ Best Green and Clean City: Boulder, Colorado

❖ Best Quirky City: Sonoma County, California

—*Modern Maturity Magazine*, 2000

If you don't yet have a vision of what your High Retirement base will be, now would be a really good time to develop one. You might want to take advantage of the northern climate in the summer and the southern climate in the winter. Maybe you'd like a very small, modest home base with a huge travel budget. And, maybe it's the home you've lived in all of your adult life with the same neighbors, church, family, and friends surrounding you.

As you narrow down this vision of your retirement home base, you'll take into account the same sort of concerns that you had earlier in life, with little twists in them. For instance, your transportation needs, earlier, were dominated by your ability to get to work and your children's ability to get to school and activities. As a retired individual, you'll still want to get around but you may want to go different places. If you're relying on a car, you'll probably have the option of avoiding rush hour. You'll be able to live somewhere that you'd never consider living if you had to fight that traffic each day. Medical care becomes more of a concern as we age, so thinking about where the doctors and hospitals are in relation to your home base is more important than it was earlier.

This is the fun part of retirement planning. Painting the picture, writing the story, making it real in your mind. Take it from a vague or generalized statement like: "We've always wanted to move out West when we retire," to a specific plan: "We'd like to buy a condo near Prescott, Arizona."

Thinking about your housing options in Low Retirement is a little less exciting, but in many ways a lot more important. You can pick a housing option for High Retirement that allows you a gradual transition into Low Retirement or you can see yourself making a transition at a specific point in time when you're no longer able to maintain your housing choice for High Retirement.

Retirement communities allow you to make this transition very gradually. Your first housing option may be an independent unit where you take care of all of your own needs. As you age, you may take advantage of the services available from the community such as prepared meals, laundry, and housekeeping. And then, as you need it, additional personalized services to help you with your activities of daily living or medical needs. Many people think this is a very comfortable option. It means they don't have to draw that line in the sand at some point in the future and move into their Low Retirement housing. Plus, they'd like to keep up their active, independent lifestyle as long as possible and only make the transition when absolutely necessary.

Are You Going to Live There Alone?

At a PTA meeting not too long ago, I sat next to an elderly woman whose daughter taught at the school. She explained that since she doesn't like to be at home after dark anymore, her daughter brought her to this event. My response was, "Oh, so you live with your daughter." I was quickly corrected: "No. She lives with me." The teacher, in her 50s, had outlived her husband and sent her children off to their own lives. She found it more logical to move back into the home she grew up in. She could care for her mother in familiar surroundings. This arrangement had obviously left her mother with a great sense of pride of ownership of her home.

Intergenerational households were the norm up through the middle of the twentieth century and are still the norm in most cultures on the planet. The notion that each generation establishes and maintains separate housing requires an economy as large and as prosperous as the United States' and other leading economies in the world.

Housing is one of the major expenses in anyone's budget. It's possible that this expectation of single family and single-generation housing is not really affordable in our economy, and that much of our anxiety about the ability of Social Security to survive and take care of us in our old age is really related to this expectation. It's not exactly true that two can live cheaper than one, but it is not double the cost for two people to live in the same dwelling as one.

Chances of Being Responsible

At one time or another, 90 percent of women become wholly responsible for their financial welfare.

—*Edward Jones Investment Services*

In some cultures, living alone is seen as a hardship and that is beginning to seep into our way of thinking as well. I'm sure you've heard someone lament, "She lives alone and doesn't have anybody." If you currently have a life partner, your chances of outliving that person are greater than 50/50, especially if they're male and if they're older than you are.

Could you maintain your planned housing after their death without their contribution to the household? When you began developing this plan, I encouraged you to do the plan both ways. 1) Assuming that your current partner's place in your life would continue into your retirement and 2) assuming that the relationship would end before retirement (whether due to death or divorce). The prudent thing would be to be ready for both scenarios.

Chances of Being Alone

Nearly 30 percent of Americans 65 years and older live alone.

Let's think about all of the other people that might end up sharing your washing machine. Let's make a list of who they are and whether they would add to your economic well-being or be an expense on your budget. There's a strong possibility, given life expectancies and given early retirement dates, that during the early years of your retirement you may have a parent or two who is still living and would need you to provide housing for them. Put them on the list if this is the case.

Your children and grandchildren might boomerang back at unpredictable intervals. Unless they are more financially sound than you are at this point, I'd put them on the list. You may have other family members, siblings, nieces, nephews, aunts, and uncles, who might also end up with you at some point. You may have a cousin you've always enjoyed who, if you pooled your financial resources and lived together, would be able to afford you much nicer housing in your retirement.

Everyone on your list will have his or her situation change many times between now and when you retire. But, thinking about them now might open up some possibilities that hadn't occurred to you before.

Possible Retirement Roommates

Name	Could Contribute	Would Cost
	$_____	$_____
	$_____	$_____
	$_____	$_____
	$_____	$_____
	$_____	$_____
	$_____	$_____
	$_____	$_____
	$_____	$_____

Another option for sharing housing involves renting out rooms in your home. Many agencies that service seniors provide roommate matching and screening services, allowing older homeowners to pay for the cost of maintaining their home through rents from individuals in need of housing. These people may be other senior citizens who are not homeowners. They might be students from a local college. They might be foreign exchange students. Or, they might be low-income individuals without the ability to finance independent housing. The idea of sharing a home with a stranger is not desirable to most older adults. But, with the help of the social workers at these agencies, many of these relationships become very positive and economically beneficial to both people.

Financial Options

When young couples come to me to discuss purchasing their first home, normally the questions on their minds are: What kind of mortgage? How much should we put down? What's our payment going to be? What kind of interest rate will we get? I usually have to put on the brakes, put all those questions aside, and ask the simple question, "Where do you want to live?"

The answer usually comes out something like, "Wherever we can afford. We just want to own a house." As we talk further, I learn that it's not really *wherever* they can afford. They really don't want to live more than 10 exits away from work. They really don't want to live on a busy street. They do have some ideas about which school districts are good. They know how much lawn they want to maintain.

Pretty quickly, I can get them to see that understanding all of their consumer preferences regarding housing is really where they need to start. I send them out to see how much their preferences cost in the real estate market, and *then* we start talking about the financial options to make that work. Because, when we buy a house, we make two purchases, we purchase the real estate and we purchase the money. In order to make your retirement choices for housing, you need to split these decisions into the same two categories. In the first two sections of this chapter we talked about where you want to live and who you want to live with you—that comes first.

Equity

Once you've decided where you want to live, we can talk about what to do with the money. In order to understand your options we need to define a little word that you've heard your whole life, and you've probably heard it misused more often than not. That word is *equity*. When you were young and people were advising you to become a homeowner, normally the encouragement included the desirability of building equity. But, they didn't just want to see you have the right to use a piece of real estate. They wanted to see your balance sheet and your net worth include the value of that piece of real estate.

Now, how does this work? When you purchase a piece of property, you also purchase the money to buy that property in the form of a mortgage. On any given day, somebody might offer you money for that property and if you want to sell it, you would need to pay back the mortgage. The difference between what the buyer gives you and what you have to turn around and give to the mortgage company is your equity.

Most people understand how this concept works with their home. But, let's apply it to other investments. Let's say that you have money invested in a 401(k) plan and you haven't paid the taxes on it. On any given day you could cash out money from that plan, in certain circumstances, and pay the taxes. The difference between what the investment company mails you and what you turn around and send to the IRS is your equity. You might also be building equity in a small business. This would be the difference between what someone would pay you to buy that business less what you owe your creditors. Accountants call this net worth, the difference between the value of an asset and the value of a liability. When you write them all down together and add them up, that becomes what they call your balance sheet.

If you have a positive balance, you own more than you owe. If you have a negative balance, you owe more than you own. Technically, this is called being bankrupt, even though very few people who are bankrupt actually file for bankruptcy protection. More and more car loans and leases have negative equity in them, meaning that the loan on the car is more than the value of the car at any given point in time. So equity is a concept we can apply to any asset and any liability at any given point in time.

Eldercare Locator Information

There are 670 Area Agencies on Aging spread across the country. Each office has a housing specialist that can assist you in your decision. To find the agency nearest you (or where you want to live) call the National Eldercare Locator toll free number at 1-800-677-1116.

Liquidity

But, back to those caring, concerned, well-meaning advisors back when you bought your first house. When they said, "We'd like to see you build up equity," what they really meant was, "We want you to build up equity *inside* your house." Let's say you told them that you were happy renting, and that the difference between what you would need to spend to purchase and maintain a home and what you're currently paying to rent, you're investing in your 401(k) plan. Then you explained that in 30 years you plan to accumulate much more equity in that plan than the equity that would have accumulated in a house. They would have looked at you like you were from some other planet.

When they started out on their path toward financial security, defined contribution plans didn't exist and homes were a wonderful investment. Since then, we've seen real estate markets go up and down. We've seen the standard deduction on our income taxes increase, making the interest deduction for home ownership less important. And, we've seen the real estate market increase choices for desirable rentals. Owning your own home affords a lot more flexibility and control for some than renting. But remember that this is separate from where you keep your equity. You may find that keeping your equity inside your home affords you peace of mind, simplicity, and a stable rate of return.

Or, you may find that keeping your equity outside your home affords you flexibility, liquidity, and more opportunities to increase that rate of return. It's not sufficient to only build up a high net worth toward retirement. It's certainly necessary and desirable, but what is sufficient is having a net worth that has a good chunk of it in liquid investments. Liquidity is measured by how quickly you can get to the money without taking a loss. Obviously, a checking account is totally liquid and a rare collectable may take years to find a buyer who is willing to pay its true value.

Your home is somewhere in between. Most housing markets in this country will sell a home in 30 to 90 days. But, the real question is, do you want to be forced to sell your home if you need cash? The answer may be yes, if you're planning to use the equity in your home to finance your final nursing home stay. At that point you wouldn't need your home anymore. But the answer might be no, if all you're looking to do is pay for ongoing expenses.

A good rule of thumb is to make sure that you have 50 percent of your total net worth invested in assets outside your home. To give you an example, if you own a $150,000 home and you've paid off your mortgage, then you have $150,000 of equity in your home. If you have, in addition to that, $150,000 of equity invested outside your home, then you have met this liquidity test. If, however, you fall into a situation more like the following: You have a paid-off home worth $120,000 and your 401(k) plan balance is $100,000, then you haven't met this test. You can also evaluate your security by adding into this analysis the present value of any pension or retirement benefits payments you're receiving. These can be added to your assets to determine the percentage of your net worth that's in your home.

Sample PV Calculation of Annuity

If you are receiving $1000 per month from a pension for life and you assume a return of 4 percent and a life expectancy of 25 then to solve for PV, enter:

❖ n = 25

❖ i = 4 (or .04 in Excel)

❖ PMT = 12000

The PV (present value) of your pension is $187,465.

This is a hard concept for most of us to grasp. We're being taught by the financial market to think in terms of payments. We shop for payments when we buy a car. We shop for payments when we buy a house. We think of our monthly retirement income as a payment. We don't often think about the values of the assets behind the car payment, the home payment, or the invested monies that our pension fund is drawing on to be able to send us that monthly income. But, much of our financial security lies in these numbers. Taking a moment to think about them and analyze them can give us a much clearer picture of whether our retirement will be secure.

Moving Equity to Gain Liquidity

So, what do you do if these numbers don't look right? You move the money around. Just like you've learned to change your investments to better match your risk tolerance and your needs regarding income and timing, you can move around your money here, too. There's a huge industry in this country ready to answer the phone and take care of it for you.

Many savings and loan companies and mortgage companies are more than happy to cash out the equity in your home without you having to sell it. Normally, they won't give you all the equity in your home without jacking up the interest rate. So, you'll be looking at being able to get out reasonably 80 to 90 percent of it at market rate. If you do this before you retire, the income from your job will be considered as the source of funds to repay the mortgage. If you do it after you retire, your retirement income will be considered your source of funds to repay. What this means is that you would probably be able to borrow more before you retire than after you retire.

You will also need to decide whether you would like to purchase a first mortgage, or keep your current first mortgage and draw out any equity that you'd like to move by using a second mortgage or a line of credit. These options allow a little more flexibility regarding repayment and interest rates. It may be exactly what you need to allow yourself the liquidity options during retirement without having the management challenges of pulling it all out up front. If you take a new first mortgage, you can take your equity and invest it in some reasonably conservative place that allows you a slightly higher return than you're paying on your mortgage. In this situation, you would almost always want to choose a variable interest rate mortgage because your investment return will vary as well, and usually vary in tandem with the mortgage interest.

Reverse Mortgages

If you're getting a little panicky, thinking about owing money on your home during your retirement, you need to go take a nice bath, relax, and skip this section. Reverse mortgages are not for the fainthearted. But in the right circumstances, they may just be the solution you are looking for.

If you absolutely know that you want to live in your home for a long time, you do not care about leaving the value of your home to your heirs, and you need additional monthly income to balance your budget, you may want to consider this option. You will be required to participate in a free counseling session before you can actually apply.

The easiest way to understand this contract is to think of it as a line of credit attached to the equity in your home, but you don't have to repay it until you (or your executor) sell your home. You can have the mortgage company send you a monthly check for life, provide you with checks to draw money when you need it or give you a lump sum up front. If the amount you have received plus the interest they have charged you is more than the value of your home, an insurance policy inside the contract pays the difference. If your home is worth more when it is sold, the difference goes to you or your estate.

There are fees for this, of course. Closing costs can vary and there is usually a monthly administrative fee. They may be financed and will incur interest as well. The interest you are charged is tied to some variable rate, like the Treasury Bill rate with an additional percentage for profit.

Reverse Mortgage Information

The Department of Housing and Urban Development (HUD) runs the Housing Counseling Clearinghouse (HCC), which can help you find a counseling office to talk about reverse mortgages at 1-800-569-4287. Households seeking additional housing information may call 1-888-HOME-4-US.

Other Ways to Finance Your Housing

Another creative way to get your equity out of your home without moving is to sell your home and lease it back from the new owner. If the new owner is a family member, you will automatically have a nice landlord. This also shifts the burden of maintenance to the new owner. There are real estate firms who specialize in this type of transaction. They represent investors who purchase rental properties and know that the best possible tenant is the previous owner.

Renting part of your home or renting your home for part of the year is another way to generate cash. You can also consider reduced rent in exchange for household maintenance duties. A local college student might be delighted to maintain your yard in return for a reduced rent. And don't forget, you're allowed to charge rent to that 28-year-old "kid" on your couch, eating your potato chips.

The Bottom Line

There are lots of decisions to make and lots of variables to consider. Use all the resources available to you to work through these decisions carefully. Your housing choice will determine much of your satisfaction in retirement.

Just ask Ellen what jobs she's had in her life and you'll get an ear-ful. "Oh honey, I've picked pig guts up off the floor, put those lit-tle plastic things on the end of shoelaces, and I even drove a cab for a while when they closed the plant. I always paid my bills, though, and sometimes, I even had a little money put back."

But ask her what she likes to do and you'll get a lecture. "What fool told you that you get to do what you like in this life? You get to do what you got to do. Don't let anybody tell you different. I never missed work except for a blizzard or something like that. And I never quit without giving notice at any job, well, except when Joe down at the shop was hitting on me and it got too hard to keep him off. The only thing that really bothered me was when these young kids would come in and be thinking they didn't have to work for a living, and I'd be doing half their work just to keep the boss from coming down on all of us. I didn't raise my kids to be like that."

Every once in a while Ellen would work for an employer that had some kind of a thrift plan. Ellen would usually sign up for it and put a little bit back every week. When she left those jobs, she wasn't really good at making sure that money got put somewhere safe, and eventually it would be spent on a car repair, or a medical bill, or a new couch. When the plant closed, she was better off than some of her friends, and she helped them out a little here and there—it was the right thing to do.

She didn't ever really see herself retiring. She just took things payday to payday and never really thought she'd live long enough to need to worry about old age. She had enough kids to live with and a sis-ter who was doing pretty well.

Doctors were telling her that her blood pressure was going too high and that maybe she should start taking it easy. She didn't know what that meant. Life had never been easy, and she wasn't really sure what they were talking about.

Her daughter's kids came to her house after school, and she rushed home every day to make sure they hadn't destroyed the place before she got there. Katie, her daughter, worked second shift, and her ex-husband wasn't paying support any more, so she couldn't afford childcare.

Ellen had just turned 62 and knew she could get a Social Security check if she wanted. She was thinking about going to work in the morning part-time so she could be home for the kids in the after-noon.

Chapter 11

Preparing for Transition

Change is never easy. Sometimes exciting, sometimes scary, but never easy. We will think about some of the changes about to happen in your relationships. You can prepare emotionally for some of the changes, but some will still be hard.

Hopes and Fears

Thinking back through the many transitions you've made in your life, what was the most exciting? A move, a new job, a new partner, becoming a parent, becoming independent, or something else? I bet if you think about the excitement that surrounded that wonderful change, you'll also remember a good deal of fear. Not knowing whether it was really going to work out or be as wonderful as you hoped, you were able to dream up lots of potential problems that helped to dampen the excitement just a little.

This transition that you're planning is no different, but may be more intense with its combination of both hopes and fears. Changing anything, even brands of pantyhose or dentists, can leave us feeling a little unsure about what might happen. You have a lot of decisions behind you at this point and one of your main jobs right now is to become comfortable with them. Take a few minutes to fill in the next two charts, allowing yourself the opportunity to see on paper what you have been dealing with emotionally.

Hopes for Retirement

Fill in as Many of the Following Blanks as You Can:

I hope _____

I hope _____

I hope _____

I hope _____

I hope _____

I hope _____

I hope _____

I hope _____

Fears for Retirement

Fill in as Many of the Following Blanks as You Can:

I fear _____

I fear _____

I fear _____

I fear _____

I fear _____

I fear _____

I fear _____

I fear _____

Look back over your two lists. Which one is longer? Did anything surprise you? Is anything missing?

Now, let's think back over the planning that you've done and see which of your hopes and fears have been addressed. Go through each item on both lists and ask yourself, "Is there anything more that I can do with my retirement plan?" Go back and address this issue. Make a list of simple actions that you can take to fill in those remaining gaps in your plan.

Transition Action Plan

List items that will help you realize your hopes and eliminate your fears. Then pick a goal date that you will try to have this item accomplished.

I plan to _____ by _____.

I plan to _____ by _____.

I plan to _____ by _____.

I plan to _____ by _____.

I plan to _____ by _____.

I plan to _____ by _____.

I plan to _____ by _____.

I plan to _____ by _____.

Friends and Family
Changing Relationships

As much as you may be looking forward to your nearing retirement date, you're probably not looking forward to breaking ties with long-term co-workers or reestablishing new relationships with family members. Remember so many years ago when you left high school and you promised your best friends that you would stay in touch? Then you found out, as life got in the way, that it was a fairly difficult thing to do. They all had their own relationships, jobs, children, and houses, many in other states. Keeping in touch became a job. It was always wonderful when you did get together, but it wasn't the same as seeing each other five days a week.

Retirement presents a very similar dynamic. Most of your co-workers will still be working, at least for a little while, and you'll have lots of freedom and time to plan activities that you would enjoy including them in. Your relationships will necessarily become more planned. Don't confuse sincerity with spontaneity. Your relationships can continue to be just as meaningful even though there are no longer spur-of-the-moment interactions and conversations. You'll probably find, however, that friendships with nonwork acquaintances will develop faster and will fill in a little of that feeling that you're missing from not being with your friends at work.

Household Adjustments

If you live by yourself, and plan to keep it that way, there won't be a lot of people adjusting to your new sleeping and eating schedule. But for most of you, you'll have people already living in your home or moving in and out of your home. Just like the adjustments that are made when a new baby comes into a home, people will be adjusting to you as you change your daily schedule. Depending upon their situation, they may or may not welcome this change. They may envy your freedom or find it hard to keep up with your new energy for finding creative and exciting adventures.

New Goals

If you planned a simultaneous retirement with your partner, then you will both be making your own personal adjustments while trying to adjust to each other. Don't expect your partner to be as excited about a hobby that you've dabbled in for 40 years and be able to catch up with you immediately. It's a great idea to find something new to both of you that you can explore together at the same speed.

You've set goals your entire life. Some you achieved, some you abandoned. You've been through goal-setting workshops at work that taught you cute sayings or complicated formulas for doing it "right." By this point you know what works for you. The only encouragement I can give you is to not stop doing it.

You may need to give yourself permission to set goals that sound a little less productive than the ones you were taught to set at work. Many of them will relate to changing your definition of who you are and what now defines your success. Your old definition won't work anymore.

The Disease of Depression

If you hold on to those old definitions too long, you may find yourself depressed. Since one in four women will develop severe depression in their lives, chances are you've been depressed before and you know that's not a pleasant place to be. I like to think about depression the way I think about colds. Some depression hangs around for a few days and goes away by itself. Some stays with you for a long time but doesn't really slow you down that much. And some can turn into a serious situation that needs medical attention. Just as with a cold, you may not run off to the doctor the first day you experience sniffles. However, be aware that if it continues beyond the time that you would normally expect a cold to go away, or if it impacts your daily functioning more than a cold would, it would be a good idea to talk to your doctor. Depression is a disease with successful treatments available. It's important that you take advantage of those treatments.

In my practice as a financial counselor, I have worked with hundreds of clients suffering with depression. Many people would say that it's understandable that a person with financial problems might be depressed. But, the more that I've worked with these individuals, I've come to understand that in the majority of the situations the depression came first and led to the financial problems. When a person is depressed, they often retreat from daily maintenance activities like opening mail, paying bills, and balancing their checking account. This can lead to chaos very quickly if left unchecked. Review the warning signs below. Be aware that depression is a fairly common disease that is rarely fatal, but often wreaks havoc on your financial life.

See how many of these symptoms are true for you:

❖ My sleeping patterns are changing.   True   False

❖ I am losing my appetite.   True   False

❖ I am not interested in anything.   True   False

❖ I'm having trouble concentrating.   True   False

❖ I'm losing interest in sex.   True   False

❖ I am anxious and worried a lot.   True   False

Talk to your doctor about these symptoms the next time you see her. Make an appointment if you circled True more than twice.

More Information on Depression

For more information about the treatment of depression, including finding a suitable therapist, see the American Psychological Association's Web page on depression at www.apa.org/pubinfo/depression.html

---

New Careers

Each day there seems to be new research coming in on the study of Alzheimer's disease. But a notion that's been around for some time is that using different parts of your brain has some preventive impact on the probability that you will develop the disease. If you're an accountant, the advice says to go take a sculpture class. If you write for a living, go take a dance class. So each time I'm required to do something that isn't comfortable because I'm not normally engaged in that activity, I chalk it up to my Alzheimer's prevention therapy program.

Even though Alzheimer's is one of the most seriously devastating illnesses we face in our later years, when I mention this strategy to people, it usually gets a laugh. The idea that doing something uncomfortable could be good for us is funny to most. We survived the exercise revolution of the '70s and '80s with its mantra, "No pain; no gain," and as women, we have certainly endured a tremendous amount of seemingly unnecessary pain for the sake of beauty.

You may have arrived at this point in your plan with the eager anticipation of a new job that is something you've always wanted to do. Or, you may have arrived at this point with the realization that your plan to not work after retirement won't be possible. The numbers didn't work out to be able to survive without supplementing your income through employment. This doesn't mean that you can't have the same eagerness and excitement surrounding your new career that others who have planned it all along are experiencing.

Working over 70

Of working women who are aged 70 or older, 25 percent work full-time.

—*AgeLine Database, 1998 American Association of Retired Persons*

Now is the time to go back to earlier visions and dreams of what you wanted to do with your life. What did you want to be when you grew up? What *do* you want to be when you grow up? Look at the number of years you have in your plan to spend in High Retirement. Chances are that's enough time for a couple of new careers.

When I was in school in the '60s, there was an unwritten rule that women who wanted to work grew up to be either teachers, secretaries, or nurses. I remember visiting my father's office and looking at the desk that his secretary had with the neat things on it. I mentally compared that to the desk my teacher had. I wondered to myself, which desk would I like to have when I grew up? And I decided that being a secretary looked more exciting than being a teacher because you got to have more cool things on your desk. (I wasn't quite sure, but I didn't think nurses got desks.)

I was one of a very small minority, at the time, whose grandmothers had both graduated from a four-year college. They were both born before the turn of the century and one was a teacher and one was a nurse. So I had been raised with the very distinct value that education was important. But that day as I chose my future career, I wondered if you were going to be a secretary, would you get to go to college.

You may have grown up with very similar messages being handed to you by your family, society, and your teachers. As I listen to women define their life's career paths, they reflect on their earlier decisions as things that just sort of happened to them. An opportunity came up that they didn't expect, or they moved with their husband at a time that wasn't advantageous. Or, they had a baby when they weren't planning, or somebody died and caused some upheaval.

When I listen to these same women describe what is happening in their later years, they use more active words to imply that they are now the ones calling the shots. Some do volunteer work for the added flexibility in scheduling or because their true passion doesn't generate economic activity that justifies a paycheck. In a way, this is a very selfish time, which allows them the freedom to nurture their true gifts. Whether your next career is to balance your emotional life or your financial life, it's an opportunity to do something you've always wanted to do. The following questionnaire can help you to narrow down what that might be. If you close in on a couple of options, why not try interning for a while? Volunteer or work for a lower wage and check it out. Tell them you'd like to hang around for 30 days and discover if this type of work is right for you.

Second Career Options

Let these questions help you narrow down the choices you will be comfortable with:

1. I want to work within _____ miles from home.
2. I want to work between _____ and _____ hours per week.
3. I want to work:

    _____ By myself

    _____ With a few people

    _____ With lots of people

4. I want to be:

    _____ Sitting down

    _____ Moving around

    _____ A little of both

5. I want to:

    _____ Learn something new

    _____ Do something I already know

6. I want to be:

    _____ Employed

    _____ Self-employed

7. I want to:

    _____ Dress up for work

    _____ Wear a uniform

    _____ Be casual

8. I need:

    _____ A lot of time off for family

    _____ A regular schedule

9. I want to work with:

    _____ Children

    _____ Adults

    _____ Both

10. I feel the happiest when I am _____.
11. I feel the most valuable when I am _____.

Take your list of preferences and call a couple of placement agencies in your area. Ask them if they have any jobs that meet your needs. If you are volunteering, use the same list when you talk to volunteer recruiters. Make sure they know what is important to you so they can help you develop a truly meaningful volunteer experience.

Multiple Roles

Women with multiple roles such as career, marriage, (grand)motherhood, and volunteer work may suffer from less depression because they have many different support sources and outlets.

—*American Psychological Association*

The Bottom Line

Gathering together all of your emotions in one place can be very difficult. Give yourself a treat for hanging in there. Having a "wait and see" attitude will catch up with you, though. Keep thinking ahead and making things happen that fulfill your vision.

Caroline hated them. She hated them more than root canals. You know, she really couldn't think of anything that she hated more. From that moment, when she opened up her first paycheck from her first job at the ice cream shop and saw that somebody had stolen half of it, to her last visit to the friendly neighborhood tax preparer, she just couldn't think of anything more annoying than taxes. She would get mad every time she saw some stupid politician making promises for some silly give-away program using her money. She loved helping people so she gave a lot of money to her church and local charities. What she didn't like was paying some joker to decide what was important.

To make matters worse, every time she had had the pleasure of interacting with the Internal Revenue Service, she would hang up believing that their pay rate must be based on how confusing and intimidating they could be. She was sure that they wrote their policies to guarantee that no one would really know what they were supposed to be doing. The more they could keep the taxpayers in the dark, the more they could keep them anxious and afraid. When she heard people talking about a kinder and gentler IRS and a taxpayer's bill of rights, she just laughed. They had all the power and they knew it.

Because of this, Caroline had always asked her employer to take out too much money from her paycheck. The last thing she wanted was to get in an argument with the IRS about owing them money. She liked the idea of investing in tax-deferred investments, but was very worried about what the IRS would do by the time those taxes came due. She loved the idea of the new Roth IRA and had put some money in one, but she really didn't trust the government to keep its promise that there wouldn't be tax on it some day.

Chapter 12

Uncle Sam Still Wants Your Money

When you add up all the taxes you pay, it's depressing. So don't do it. Instead, learn how each one is calculated and what you can do to pay the least amount for your situation.

What's Taxed and What's Not

And now—the chapter you've all been waiting for. Before I sound too unpatriotic, let me explain that without taxes, life as you know it would go away very quickly. There are things in this country that we all take totally for granted that are only possible because of our relatively efficient taxation system.

There are certainly lots of aspects of the income tax system that could be improved. I don't think they could have made it more complicated if they had set out with that as their only goal. But what has happened is that the income tax is not only a tool for collecting revenue to fund the business of our government, it has also become a way to control your behavior—our collective behavior that we call our economy.

The girls in my Girl Scout troop have developed a wonderful skill. They have refined to perfection the ability to notice, report, and complain about things that aren't fair. Eleven out of thirteen are first-born children. We first-borns know that the world is supposed to behave exactly as we decide. We know this with total certainty. Those of you who are farther down the birth order can attest to the fact that your oldest siblings have it all figured out.

In Scout Leader training they teach us to build on the girls' strengths. So I have installed a new rule in our troop. Each time we get together, we have to come up with at least 10 things that aren't fair about that event. We've had a great deal of fun playing this game and in the process have learned the valuable lesson that no matter how hard we try, there are still going to be lots of things that just don't come out fair. The girls and I would like to invite you to become honorary members of our troop for the rest of this chapter and play this game with us.

By now you've gotten really used to knowing what after-tax income looks like. Caroline was shocked, just like all of us were, the first time we saw that picture. We worked 10 hours at $2.00 an hour and expected a paycheck of $20. When the paycheck said $13.50, we were sure there must have been a mistake (especially since we had already picked out a nice outfit for, you guessed it, $20). But if, instead, we took that $13.50 and we put it in an investment that qualified as an individual retirement account, years later when we take it out, the $13.50 won't be taxed again. When the investment company sends us a check for $270, we only need to pay tax on the other $256.

There's another sneaky thing that's going on here. The $256 really has the purchasing power of about $60 compared to the $13.50 that you originally invested. But, you're not only paying taxes on the real amount of that investment, you're also paying taxes on the inflation that happened to those dollars during that time that your money was invested.

The tax rate that you will pay on the $256 is your marginal tax rate the year that you withdraw the money from the IRA. Depending upon where you are in the tax brackets, that withdrawal could move you into the next higher tax bracket and therefore the withdrawal would be taxed at the next bracket's rate.

Understanding what tax bracket you're in continues to be important, as I explain the difference between ordinary tax rates and capital gain tax rates. A capital gain is what happens when you buy something and it increases in value before you sell it. This is different than loaning money to someone and having them pay you interest on that loan.

Capital Gains Arguments

A capital gain happens when a stock or other asset, like your home, is sold at a price that is higher than when it was purchased. The amount of the gain may be subject to capital gains taxes. Congress argues about this taxation strategy every chance they get. Some say it deters investment and growth in the economy. Others say that it only taxes the rich, so it's a good way to raise money. They have agreed recently that the gain in your residence should probably not be taxed (unless you haven't lived there much or you have a very large gain).

Look at the following chart and find your marginal tax bracket and then identify your capital gain tax bracket. The interesting thing is that if you place an investment in a tax-deferred account like an IRA or 401(k), and that investment grows in value, it would have a capital gain. But, because it's tax-deferred, you will pay ordinary income tax rates when you cash it out. If it hadn't been tax-deferred, you would pay the capital gains tax rates.

Capital Gains Tax Rates

If You Are in the 15 Percent Tax Bracket:

Asset held for 1 yr.	Asset held for 5 yrs.
10%	8%

If You Are Above the 15 Percent Tax Bracket:

Asset held for 1 yr.	Asset held for 5 yrs.
20%	18%

The general rule that should be pretty easy to remember is that if you paid the tax before you put the money into the investment, you don't pay the tax when you take that money out of the investment. You will pay tax on the earnings that your investment enjoys. If you didn't pay the tax on the money as it went in, then the entire investment will be taxed when you take it out at retirement. It will be taxed at your marginal tax rate for the year when you make the withdrawal. Accounts that fall under these general rules include traditional IRA's, Simplified Employee Pension (SEP) IRA's, KEOGH (self-employment) Pension Plans, Defined Benefit Plans, Defined Contribution Plans, Tax Deferred Annuities, and 401(k)/403(b) Plans.

Of course, every rule has its exceptions. The first one I will mention is the Roth IRA, which allows you to take money out totally tax-free if you wait five years from the date of your first contribution, if you are over $59^{1}/_{2}$ years old.

State and Federal Employees

If you are covered by either the state or federal retirement systems, your benefits are mostly taxable to you. Your plan administrators can give you an estimate of how much may be exempt from taxes.

The really big exception to this rule is the way that Social Security benefits are now taxed. When you contribute money to the Social Security system, you have already paid income tax on those contributions. You have not paid tax on the portion that your employer pays in, which is equal to your portion. You are not taxed on the earnings of your money during your working years. So, if this follows the normal rule, you would not be paying tax on your contribution at retirement and you would pay tax on your employer's contribution and the earnings it's enjoyed.

But because Social Security was seen by many as a social welfare system, it brought out tremendous cries when Congress determined that it should be taxable. So, instead of following the normal rules, they figured out a sliding scale based on other income you receive to determine how much, if any, of your Social Security benefits are subject to income tax during retirement.

Taxation of Social Security Benefits

To determine whether you will need to pay federal income tax on your Social Security benefits, first add up your 1) earnings; 2) tax-exempt interest; and 3) half of your Social Security benefits. If this number is less than $25,000, if you're single; or $32,000, if you're married, you're clear. No tax. Over those amounts an increasing percentage (up to 85 percent) will be taxed at your regular tax rate.

One situation to be careful of is what happens in years when you take a distribution from a retirement plan. Whether you intend to spend that money or reinvest it in a taxable investment, that will increase your taxable income for that year and sometimes cause your Social Security benefits to incur tax. (Did I hear a "Not fair"?)

Social Security Benefits

The progressive benefit provides a higher replacement rate for workers with lower earnings. For the median female retiree, Social Security replaces 54 percent of average lifetime earnings, compared with 41 percent for the median male.

Tax Planning Strategies

Avoid Penalties

We've all had some personal interaction with the speeding laws at some point in our lives. But, I bet you never got a ticket for going too slow. The police don't get a lot of opportunity to pass out tickets for that crime. Well, the retirement police give out tickets for going too fast *and* too slow. If you go too fast and take your money out before age 59$^1/_2$, the ticket is $10 (per $100 of withdrawals). If you go too slow, and don't start taking your money out by 70$^1/_2$, your ticket goes up to $50 (per $100 of withdrawals).

Brace yourselves. The IRS actually made something simpler a couple of months ago. The rules for how much you had to take out beginning at 70$^1/_2$ were so complicated that even financial planners hated figuring it out. Now, most of you will use a uniform table that assumes a joint life expectancy recalculated annually for a designated beneficiary 10 years younger than you are. You can use this table regardless of whether you've named a beneficiary or your beneficiary, such as your spouse, is older than you are. These new rules generally result in smaller required withdrawals, which will allow you to leave more money in your IRA or 401(k) and continue to minimize your taxes.

Diversify Taxes

It may not be as awful as Caroline thinks it is, but there is always a risk that the tax laws will change and that assumptions you have made will no longer be in your best interest. We learned that when you diversify or pick different types of investments, you can minimize certain types of risks in those investments.

The same logic holds true with tax strategies. If you diversify the tax status of your various investments, you can minimize the impact that any future changes in the tax code will have on you. Most people arrive at retirement having done this unconsciously. They will have some of their money in government pensions or Social Security, some of their money in employer pensions, some in defined contribution accounts, and some in individual tax-deferred accounts, and other monies in accounts where they have already paid the tax.

If the tax is already deferred, it's a good idea to keep deferring it until the time when penalties become a problem. So, if you have enough investments that you've already paid the tax on, that you can draw from, say from age 65 to age $70^1/_2$, then do that first. At $70^1/_2$, when you're required to begin withdrawing tax-deferred money, then switch to the tax-deferred accounts.

Remember that the underlying investment and the tax status of the investment are two different things. You may own an investment that you thoroughly love and don't want to cash it out, but it becomes necessary to do this because of the withdrawal rules and the high penalties. Usually, with minimal transaction fees, you can turn that investment into cash, thereby fulfilling the IRS rules and turn right around and purchase it again, this time with after-tax money, thereby fulfilling your investment preference.

After-Tax Investments

Investments that you own, whether individual or pooled into mutual funds, will be taxed if they make you money. They will reduce your taxes if they don't make you money. There are two ways that those taxes are calculated. The first is fairly simple, you receive the dividend or interest paid to you during a tax year and at the end of the year that company sends you a "1099" stating how much income you had. You add this to your "1040" on Schedule B if your income from all dividends and interest is more than $400 in any tax year. You will pay your normal marginal tax rate on that income.

This is due when you file your taxes on April 15 unless you owe more than $1000. In this case, you will need to file quarterly estimates, which look sort of like loan payment coupons. All they have on them is your name, your Social Security number, and the amount of money you're sending in. If this is the first year that you were required to pay quarterly estimates, you can probably skate by without much interest or penalty if you file it at the end of the year. The next year you merely need to pay estimates equal to 28% of your previous year's tax liability in order to stay clean with the IRS. Then in April, you can send in any difference. This rule allows you the freedom to not have to calculate your actual income and tax liability each quarter throughout the year.

The second way the taxes are calculated on investment earnings is through the capital gains tax. To understand capital gains, you need to know two things. First, you need to know what you paid for it (this number is called your *basis* in that asset) and second, you need to know what you sold the investment for. The difference between the selling price and your basis is your gain. The capital gains tax is the percentage you figured out earlier in the chapter that will be applied to that gain.

Sample Capital Gains Calculation

Let's say that 10 years ago, you bought 100 shares in a start-up technology company. You spent $1,000. Yesterday you sold those shares for $3,000. You are in the 28 percent marginal tax bracket, so your capital gains rate is 20 percent. Your gain is $2,000. $2,000 X 20 percent = $400 tax you owe.

Knowing what your basis is in an investment is probably the most difficult piece of information to keep track of, especially if you are purchasing shares of a mutual fund monthly. Since most funds make distributions on an ongoing basis, you will pay taxes each year on those earnings, even if you reinvest your earnings. This causes your basis to go up each year. One of the things that you can ask your broker, your mutual fund company, your financial planner, or your banker is whether they can do this for you. Ask them what type of information they provide to allow you to keep the records. Have them show you what it looks like and make sure you understand it before you begin selling these investments and are then forced to file the appropriate tax returns.

Other Tax Issues

Since all states, territories, counties, cities, school districts, and other governmental entities have different practices regarding collection of revenues necessary to do business, it's important that you become very familiar with the governments that have a right to collect taxes from you. Some states have very high income taxes and some have none.

Taxation in Different States

Local libraries and many Web sites collect up-to-date information on the income tax strategies in all the states. You can also call that state's treasurer to receive information and a tax return form. This would allow you to see how their laws would affect you.

Some areas will fund their school systems through property taxes and some will levy income taxes. Some cities and counties have their own income tax, but many don't. You may or may not be familiar with a type of tax sometimes called a personal property tax, or intangible property tax. This is a tax that works very much like the real estate taxes you pay but it's levied against non-real estate assets like mutual funds, stocks, bonds, and other investments.

If you know what place you're going to retire, it's easy enough to call a tax preparer in that area and ask them which governments will be taxing you when you live there and ask them to send you sample tax returns from those governments. Take the numbers that you've projected to have throughout your retirement years and do some mock tax returns rather than guess as to the amount of your taxes. This level of investigation will leave you without any surprises come tax time.

Remember that real estate taxes are often voted an increase, but are also adjusted automatically for increases in the value of the real estate. So, as you do your budget projections throughout retirement, take that into account. Many states have begun programs to help senior citizens to reduce or defer their property tax liability. If you need more money to make sure that you'll be able to stay in your home, this may be an option available to you.

So, how many things did you find that weren't fair? If you didn't find 10, you may need to go back and read it again—you may not have been paying total attention. The main thing that isn't fair is that, as much as you ask other people for guidance, they're still your taxes to pay and your penalties to pay if you make a mistake. So be aware and ask questions. If you can't afford a paid tax preparer, there are community agencies, and even the IRS itself, who will help you make sure that you're following the rules and paying the least amount of tax.

The Bottom Line

As important as taxes are in your budget, do not run your life around them. Keep your values and goals primary and then learn how you can achieve the best tax treatment of your income and investments that meet those goals.

When Elizabeth lost her husband, twenty-five years ago, the mortgage life insurance had paid off the mortgage and she put his life insurance from work in a bond fund to save for the kids' education. Without the mortgage payment and with his Social Security survivor benefits, her income was reasonable to raise the kids. They had to change their big vacations to little ones and thrift stores became a regular stop during shopping trips. But she never touched the life insurance money.

As the kids reached college age, she divided the money into three accounts and taught each of them how to make withdrawals and how to apply for student loans to make up the difference. She explained that it was all there was, and that they needed to choose a college that they could afford.

As soon as the kids were out of the house, she adjusted to the loss of the Social Security income and still managed to increase her contribution to her retirement funds. She actively managed her investment choices so that she could retire on time.

What she didn't know how to do, was take money out. All of her children thought it was pretty cool that she involved them in the management of their college funds. What they didn't know was that she was delegating the task that caused her tremendous anxiety.

Ever since her husband died, she clung to the balances in her different investment accounts as her security. This money was as close as she was going to come to replacing the comfort that her husband had provided her when he was living.

So at 65, she still lived in the paid-off home that her husband's death afforded her. She was organized beyond belief. She had all the forms and documents and files she needed to move into her High Retirement without a care.

The first few months of her retirement were an adjustment financially. The combined income from her Social Security benefits and her company's defined benefit plan gave her about 75 percent of her pre-retirement income. She was a good budgeter and she knew there was no need for her to tap into her investments. She'd just be careful and make every penny count.

One day, she came home from the museum and her answering machine light was on. It was her youngest daughter, "Mom, the baby's coming early. I want you to be here. Dan will pick you up. Call us with your flight number." She couldn't make herself buy the plane ticket and she knew she needed help.

Chapter 13

Paying Attention Pays Off

The good news is: You have assets to manage. The bad news is: You have to manage them. It's not as complicated as it might seem, before you try it. I'll walk you through the key decisions and help you line up your advisors.

Managing Your Own Investments

If you've come this far in your retirement planning and you're still worried about outliving your money, give your friendly insurance agent a call and find out all the things that can lower your life expectancy. Some of them are pretty exciting like race-car driving, sky diving, mountain climbing, and scuba diving. Others may achieve the same goal but might not be consistent with your lifestyle: smoking, unsafe sex, and drunk driving come to mind. Dying earlier would certainly solve your problems. Unfortunately, you can't even count on the above list of danger-ous behaviors to do the trick.

So, it's probably a better strategy to just get used to the fact that you're going to be around for a while. By now, you should have a pretty clear picture of what money you have coming in, and what funds you have invested to supplement that income. The decisions that you've made before retirement may have been right or wrong, but they're made. And now you have a new task of approaching your High Retirement period with confidence and attention.

Women's Life Expectancy

Women need more savings because they tend to live longer than men. On average, a woman who reaches age 65 will live another 19 years compared with 15 years for a man.

—*USA Today,* 1999

I'm always amazed at the never-ending talent humans have to take fairly simple things and make them complicated. Nine chapters ago we talked about the fact that there are really only five things you can do with your money, and when we talk about investments during retirement, we're narrowing it down to three of those.

1. Keep it as cash.

2. Loan it to someone.

3. Buy something you keep.

But the names and numbers and legalese that gets thrown around to define the millions of choices you have within these three options can get pretty intense. Just as you made changes in your asset allocations approaching retirement, now that you're retired you'll want to change that again.

The biggest difference now is your need for cash. Let's say that you have determined that you need $400 per month to balance your budget. One relatively calm way to think about managing your money is to take that $400 and multiply it by 24 months. Let's round that up to $10,000. You may already have this amount of money in cash, meaning money markets, CDs, or savings accounts, but if you don't, you can take after-tax money and move it to a money market.

Each month you have your financial institution transfer $400 from your money market into your household checking account. This begins to look like another pension check. You add that to your Social Security and other retirement checks and you have your monthly income that you then manage just as you did when you were managing a paycheck.

You may have a short-term statement savings account where a portion of your monthly income goes to fund short-term periodic needs, like emergency plane tickets. You would have all dividends and interest earnings on your various investments paid into your money market, then every six months you would take a look at the balance in that money market and if it's dropped below $10,000, you would liquidate another investment. If your earnings during that six-month period were enough to keep the balance stable, then you need not cash out anything.

Each year, you would want to give yourself a cost of living adjustment in your draw from this fund equal to the same adjustment that you get from Social Security. If you think that the $400 is using up your money too quickly, then something's wrong with your underlying assumptions. Go back to your present value calculations for your current age, your current balance in your investments, and your current interest or earnings assumptions and see if the numbers work. If they don't, then your options are dying earlier, spending less, or investing at a higher rate of return.

If you have taken an early retirement and have good genes, you may be looking at a retirement period that is longer than the time you spent working full-time. A retirement period of 25 or 30 years will see a lot of fluctuations in the financial markets. If you follow the above formula, which has you keeping two years' worth of your needs in cash, you should be able to ride out most time periods when the value of your investments drop.

I'm going to assume that right now, today, you are as competent as you have ever been at managing your investments and that you continue to have the capacity to learn and understand more complicated topics. I'm also going to assume that at some point during your Low Retirement you will begin to lose either your competency or your capacity to continue learning. This may be due to memory problems or general physical deterioration and other problems. It's hard to tell you how you will know when this starts to happen. Our normal reaction is to become very defensive and hold on to the control and the power that we've enjoyed up to that point.

Women Are More Conservative

Even when women do save for retirement, they tend to save less and invest more conservatively than men. As a result, single women are on track to have a much smaller retirement income than single men and couples.

—*The WEFA Group for Oppenheimer Management*

Just like the housing decisions that you thought through, the investment management decisions may need to take a couple of different forms. There are many options and strategies for you to pick from to make sure that this transition is comfortable for both you and those around you.

The one option that I want you to avoid is that of a guardianship. A guardianship is what happens when you fail to plan for a time when you can no longer manage your own finances. It is an expensive and painful process to put into place for both you and the person who becomes your guardian. Your attorney can help you draft documents using one of various strategies that will rationally transfer the control of your financial assets to someone else. She might advise that you use a trust or a Power of Attorney or other legal strategies.

Who, What, When, Where, and Why?

Some things in your life you manage totally and completely and will not let anyone else have any say in the matter. Thanksgiving dinner might be like this at your house. The stuffing is the way the stuffing has been for 40 years and no one dares to tell you to do it differently.

For other things in your life you may rely totally on someone else's judgment, timing, and expertise. Your dentist calls to remind you it's time for your check up and you rely totally on her judgment to determine when you need additional work done to your teeth.

You might take a middle ground with your car. You check around for deals on oil changes, you let your brother-in-law do preventive maintenance, but when major systems have a problem, you'll only trust the dealer.

As you think about how you're going to manage your investments, you may want to think about your comfort level as it relates to the way that you manage other challenges in your life. Do you think about your investments the way you think about your teeth—you can't read those x-rays and you don't want to learn? Or, do you think about your investments the way you think about your car—you like the class you took at the local community college in car maintenance and you enjoy getting a good deal on your repairs?

There's another issue that's rather difficult to think about. When we talk about the concept of trust, you need to ask yourself how much *you* trust *you*. We've already agreed that as you age you're likely to become more of who you are, not somebody new. If you have seen yourself spend windfalls in the past faster than you expected, or you became dependent upon credit cards throughout your life, this may contribute to your fear about losing your money. It's never too late to work on the underlying emotional issues that lead to the types of overspending that can impact your security.

But, you may want to consider certain financial and legal strategies that can protect your assets while you're working on your behavior. Many financial products are sold using this very notion. You know people who cannot keep a dime in a savings account, but will make an extra payment on a mortgage, or will pay the premium for their whole life insurance knowing that there's a savings element in that contract. These two bills that come in the mail are hidden savings that some people find comfortable to fund because they know they can't get to the money. If you are likely to undermine your own security, the sooner you acknowledge that and put into motion strategies where you can protect yourself, the better off you'll be.

As you think through all of the issues that are important in how you manage your money during retirement, it might be helpful for me to reduce them to five "W" questions: Who, what, when, where, and why.

1. *Who* will be selecting the investment?
2. *What* will they be buying?
3. *When* will it be taxed?
4. *Where* will it be held?
5. *Why* are they buying it?

As we sort through these five questions, you'll begin to see most of the decisions that you'll be asked to make as you manage your investments.

Who

Who makes your investment decisions? It can be a variety of individuals. It's important that you understand your options and that you leave as many of them open as possible. The only one you want to avoid, as I stated, is a guardian. A guardian is a person who petitions the Court to take over responsibility for you and your assets. This normally only happens when you have shown the inability to do it yourself, either due to physical or mental incapacity. I've never met a guardian who was having a good time. Do everyone you love a favor and make sure that you structure your finances in a way that doesn't force them to have to do this at some point in the future.

Now let's get back to the options that are a good idea. The first one, of course, is you. With the right attitude, enough attention, and some desire to keep learning and exploring the options available to you, you can be the best manager that your money can have. You are the one who cares the most about it, and presumably, has the most to lose if mistakes are made.

Being the manager doesn't mean that you don't consult with experts and advisors when you feel the need. Most retirees with invested assets will hire a CPA or tax preparer to help them through the cumbersome task of filing their income tax returns to the various governments. I've already advised you on several occasions to consult with an attorney for various legal documents that will impact your financial security.

You might choose to use a professional financial planner to help you design a comprehensive financial plan. The type of planner I'm referring to is one who would charge you either by the hour or with a flat fee to do a complete data gathering and analysis, which would lead to a set of recommendations for you to follow in all the aspects of your financial life. Their training and expertise can often identify problems and locate solutions very efficiently.

If you have followed the steps that I have outlined in this book though, and gone through many of the issues I've raised, you have already done much of the work that a financial planner would offer you. You might be much better off to pay an hourly fee, knowing that you've already collected much of the data and done some of the analysis. Planners are very accustomed to working with people who are totally disorganized and need lots of help gathering information.

I would also add to the list of effective advisors, psychologists and clinical social workers who can help you work through the fears, anxieties, and relationship issues that will impact your financial security. Much of what I'm recommending involves good communication patterns with family members. If those relationships are strained, it's often helpful to bring a counselor or mediator into the problem-solving process.

The other option you have is to delegate these decisions to someone else. Your choices include an asset manager, a trustee, or a family member. Financial planners often are also doing business as asset managers. The difference is that the planner creates the plan, the asset manager controls and manages the assets in the plan. Asset managers charge a yearly fee equal to a percentage of the assets that they're managing. This might be anywhere from $3/4$ to $1^1/2$ percent of the assets that you place in their custody.

You might also choose to place the assets in a trust and appoint a trustee to manage them for you. You can start off as the trustee and appoint a successor trustee to take over when you become unable to manage. Trustees can be banks, attorneys, family members, or anyone you feel has the skills to do this. You might also pass the responsibility to a family member by giving them a Power of Attorney without creating a trust.

Uncertainty in Selecting an Advisor

Despite the millions of dollars now being expended in an effort to reach women investors, women still lack the information needed to manage their finances. Fifty percent of those who had not consulted a financial professional said they did not know how to select one.

As you evaluate these options and think about what will work best for you, remember that you can change your decision as long as you're still competent. You might start out doing it yourself with the help of your CPA and attorney, then move your assets to an asset manager at some point, following that with a Power of Attorney given to a family member, and ending up with a trust that protects you in your final years.

What

We've pretty much beaten this one to death so I won't bore you again. What you buy will be a financial tool that will either be cash, a loan to someone, or a piece of something. Depending upon who you trust to pay you the return that you desire and what type of risk you're willing to take, you will have thousands of choices for what you invest in.

Women As Investors

Women are thoughtful investors! Women tend to conduct thorough research before investing and often look at the "whole picture" and opportunities an investment may provide, thoroughly analyzing decisions they make with their money. Women also tend to follow a consistent, long-term approach to investing and typically purchase stocks of well-known consumer companies that have proven profitable from the sale for their goods or serviced to the public.

—*National Association of Investors Corporation*

When

When each investment will be taxed is a critical piece of the management job that you or someone has to do. If you deferred taxes on that investment, you will need to understand the tax rules we covered in the last chapter and keep accurate records to be able to file appropriate returns. This is one of those questions that you can ask as you determine who's going to manage the money. Find out who is responsible for keeping records of the basis of each investment. This can be an irritating piece of information to hold on to. If an asset manager tells you they will do it for you, that might add value to their services.

Where

Several years ago I was working with a woman, blind since birth, who had lived her entire adult life on about $500 a month from a government disability program. Since she was enrolled in Medicaid, she was forbidden to have money in the bank over about $1,500. It never struck me as odd that, even though she had been blind her entire life, she had a nice bookshelf full of books in her apartment.

I was helping her to set up her accounting system for a small business she was starting and she needed a piece of software that her rehabilitation program wouldn't buy for her. She sent me to her bookshelf and told me to bring her back, *The Complete Works of Mark Twain*. She had hollowed out the pages and stored several hundred dollars in cash. Later, I learned that she had saved $20 a week her entire adult life of 15 years and had over $15,000 stored in those books. She explained to me that she felt very vulnerable living on the income that she had and she didn't trust the government to continue her income without interruption. The only way she knew how to make herself feel more secure was to save money. Her fake book collection was the only place she was allowed to save.

Thankfully, you have a few more options to consider. It's important that we don't confuse the *where* with the *who*. Money can be deposited with your employer's pension fund, a mutual fund company, an insurance company, the government, or a stockbroker, but that has nothing to do with who is managing it. These two decisions are separate.

When you leave your employer, your 401(k) plan may allow you to leave money on deposit in their funds. This doesn't mean that your employer is managing your 401(k) money. You could also take that money and transfer it, keeping it in the same mutual fund but moving it to a brokerage account. Again, this doesn't mean that your broker is managing your money. Your broker may give you information on different investments and may encourage you to conduct certain trades of investments, but brokers are not managers and the converse is true—asset managers are not brokers.

Why

Earlier in your life you had lots of reasons why you might invest: purchasing a home, educating children, weathering a layoff, etc. Your reasons to invest in retirement are slightly different.

You are primarily interested in managing your cash flow. Making sure you can take care of your needs throughout the remainder of your life is your primary concern. You may also want to preserve your assets to be able to leave an estate for your children or a charity.

If you first know why you are investing, it makes it much easier to select the appropriate investment. We talked earlier about having two years of your cash needs in cash. You may want to extend this to three if you think that the next down cycle in the stock market would last longer than three. Or you may want to have the next two years of your assets in investments, like highly rated bonds, that aren't dependent upon the fluctuations in stock prices.

Beyond that, most experts would agree that you are making "long-term" investments and can absorb more risk with your money. And money that you intend to leave in your estate is certainly "long term" because your heirs can leave it in the investments you select, with the possible exception of those you have not yet paid income tax on.

So, the answer to the why question is mostly tied to the timing of when you will need that chunk of your money, if ever. And whether you intend to have it generate income or be cashed in at some point.

The Bottom Line

Even if you break out in hives thinking about the mere idea of managing your own investments, you will still have several very important decisions to make. Ask a lot of questions. Don't be afraid to appear stupid. This is new to you and you're allowed to take your time learning it.

Maria's husband died 20 years ago after a productive career at a manufacturing plant in their small town. Maria had worked there on and off during her life but never built up retirement benefits. His pension and her half of his Social Security had been enough to allow her to live comfortably in their modest home, which he had paid off before he died.

But Puerto Rico was a long way from New Jersey where her two sons had landed after college. They both did something with computers, she wasn't sure what, and she couldn't stand the things until the day that a picture of her new great-grandbaby showed up on her computer screen. She had never liked to drive very much, but at 82 she was now without a license due to her failing eyesight and some shaking she had developed in her right arm.

Her sons would come visit her often, but their wives were beginning to complain about the travel expenses. It was time for her to move to New Jersey. It was a long process to actually get her moved. Selling her home took some time. Helping her pack and get rid of items she couldn't bring with her, finding new doctors and services in their town all took time.

She was not the most willing participant in this transition. Her anxiety about changing climates, changing churches, having to use English more, and leaving her home of 50 years was totally understandable. But, she was having trouble remembering to take her medicine and her sons knew it was only going to get worse.

It also took time to find housing that she would enjoy. They settled on an independent living efficiency apartment in a retirement community near their neighborhood. Both of their wives worked and their children were busy with their own families. People were rarely home at their houses to be able to care for Maria. They felt she would be better off in a community where she could establish relationships and have immediate care when she needed it.

They looked at the cost and decided that they would split the difference after what Maria could afford. They invested the $30,000 they got from selling her home as an emergency fund and then they very carefully charted out a calendar to make sure that someone stopped by every day.

Chapter 14

If You're Lucky

If you're lucky, you'll live a long time. But living a long time may mean needing extensive care before you die. There are many more options today than 50 years ago. Your job is to plan for the one that is comfortable to you.

Family-Based Care

Let's be honest. None of us are going to be that much fun to take care of when we get old. Pick an adjective that describes one of your least attractive personality traits today. Then fast forward 20 years and put the word *very* in front of it. If you are particular today, you'll be *very* particular in 25 years. If you are impatient today, you will be *very* impatient in 30 years. If you are judgmental today, you will be *very* judgmental in 35 years. Social workers talk about a concept called the *continuity of aging*. People don't usually make big left, right, or "U" turns as they get older. They normally continue on the same path with increasing intensity.

The same notion can be applied to relationships. If you don't get along with one of your offspring or one of your siblings now, don't expect that someday when you're sick and need care that those relationships will be miraculously healed.

The statistics tell us that 80 percent of older adults who require daily care are receiving that care from family members. Only 20 percent are receiving the care from professional nurses and other paid caregivers. An extremely common phrase in our culture is, "I don't want to be a burden to my children." But, looking at these numbers, it appears as though it takes a great deal of effort to not end up in that situation. Certainly there are family caregivers that wouldn't describe their efforts as burdens, but most people receiving the care feel that guilt.

Parental Care

Women ages 53 to 65 who spend at least two hours per week, on average, helping their parents with personal care or with chores and errands cut back their hours of paid work by 43 percent.

—*Study: Parental Care at Midlife, Urban Institute*

As you work through your retirement plan, you may come to realize that this type of care may be the only economic or feasible way for you to get your needs met during your Low Retirement period. Rather than denying that it will have to happen, it would be much better to approach it in the same planful way that you've approached many other decisions we've covered in this book.

I'm going to give you an example in reverse to illustrate the value in this. Several years ago I was meeting with a family for a financial counseling session. The father was a truck driver and the mother was a stay-at-home mom of three children, ages one to seven. The father's income as an independent owner-operator was $55,000 after the expenses of maintaining his truck.

He had no disability insurance. Truck drivers have a very hard time purchasing disability insurance because of the nature of their work. If they do find it, insurance companies charge them very high premiums. Because this family was in a financial bind to begin with, I was concerned that even a short-term disability would throw them over the edge.

I asked him what he felt would happen if he weren't able to work due to a disability. I got a very quick and clear response, "My mother would never let my children go hungry." To check the veracity of this assumption, I picked up the phone on the desk and handed it to him and asked him if his mother knew that she was his disability policy. I said, "Let's call her and make sure that her plans are consistent with your needs." I then learned that she had just sold her family home and moved into a two-bedroom condo in Florida. Clearly she was not *planning* for five people to move in from five states away.

My eight-year-old tells me all the time that I'm going to live with her when I'm old and wrinkled. I'm predicting this invitation will be withdrawn around the time she's 13. Certainly you may have family members who would be delighted to have you live with them as you age. Families are the backbone of our culture. It is totally acceptable and wonderful to spend your final years with people you love. My encouragement is to begin that conversation before you need round-the-clock care, letting everyone know your preferences while learning what their needs are.

Home Health Care

Even the most loving and attentive of family members may not have the skills to do complicated medical procedures. And no one has the ability to stay up round the clock, except new mothers, of course. Consumers have demanded, and the market has responded with a wide range of services that are available in your own home.

A quick peek at your Yellow Pages directory under "Home Health Services" will reveal a wide variety of services that can be mixed and matched to take care of your unique needs. Caregivers range from companions who are there "just in case," to registered nurses, therapists, and mobile medical technicians.

The question always comes back to cost, however. These are the types of services that your Long-Term Care Insurance would cover if you elect to purchase a rider for home health care. The Medicaid program pays for some services through a program designed to keep people from entering nursing homes. It is much more cost-effective to care for a person in their own home in many cases. And you can always pay cash for these services.

There are many community services available through the Area Agencies on Aging. A caseworker from the office that serves your county can meet with you and discuss access to the types of services you need. You may have heard of the Meals on Wheels programs, but this is only one of many services available to senior citizens. There may be shopper services, transportation to doctor appointments and housecleaning available. The national number to call to locate the agency in your area is 1-800-677-1116. There are hundreds of these agencies in the country. They are central clearinghouses for all programs in the community that service our aging population. They administer some programs and refer to others.

Female Caregivers

More than 7 in 10 caregivers are female.

—American Association of Retired People

Another way to get services in your own home is to choose a home where the services are included. This relatively new package is called assisted living. This is a general term for living arrangements where residents live independently but have services, such as cooking and laundry, available to them. They can remind you to take your medicine, take you to the doctor and clean your house. This sounds fabulous! Where do I sign up? Now!

Nursing Homes

Half of us will spend some time in a nursing home before we die. Now all we have to do is figure out if it will be you or me. And one of us doesn't have to read this section. I've just decided that it's you, so you need to read on.

I want you to spend at least as much time on this part of your planning as you spent planning your daughter's wedding, your first wedding, or your last vacation. This is important. And you're the one who will be most affected by the plan, so don't leave it up to a family member when it's too late for you to be involved. Most nursing home choices are made by rushed family members in the middle of a crisis, as the hospital is trying to put someone else in your bed.

Alzheimer's Care Period

Alzheimer's can last from 3 to 20 years after the onset of symptoms, and the average duration is 8 years.

—*Administration on Aging*

Let's get one thing out of the way right now. You don't want to go into a nursing home. You know it. I know it. Everyone in your family knows it. Tell me something they don't know. Like, the day you absolutely have to go into a care facility, which one do you want to go to? Saying you don't want to go, over and over, does absolutely nothing to help your loved ones know what to do when all other options have been exhausted.

You've learned to accept a lot of unpleasant things in your life. And you are absolutely sure that this would be extremely unpleasant. But, if you plan other items well, you may be able to stay in your home and receive services there. Remember, you have a 50 percent chance that whatever kills you will do it quickly and you won't have the need for these services at all. Joyful thought, isn't it.

Nursing Home Expenditures

Nursing home care expenditures increased from $17.4 billion in 1970 to $84.7 billion in 1998.

—*Health Care Financing Administration, 1998 Expenditures*

Since we are assuming you are the half of the two of us that will be using these services, you need to go shopping. Oh, not again! Take some friends and make a party out of it. Make some treats and surprise the nursing home residents with something special. Find some way to make this rewarding. But do it.

The Elder Care Locator 1-800-677-1116 can give you a list of all the facilities in the area where you plan to retire. You might start at the Continuing Care Retirement Communities (CCRC's) in your area. These are facilities that provide a variety of levels of care, from independent living to nursing home care. If you move in when you are still active, you may be required to enter their nursing home when you need care, so check it out first. If you wouldn't want to end up there, don't start out in one of their other units.

There are over 15,000 certified nursing homes in the country. There are over 600 Long-Term Care Ombudsman programs in the country. Current phone numbers for each state are at www.medicare.gov and in directory assistance. Their volunteers visit nursing homes regularly to check out the care offered. They can help you identify facilities that may be right for you.

Once you have your list of possible facilities, begin narrowing down your needs. Things that might be important to you are:

- ❖ Location: Do you want to be close to family? Who will be your advocate as you become older?
- ❖ Availability: How long is their waiting list? Should you get on it now?
- ❖ Staffing: Who works there? What are their licenses? How are they screened?

❖ Medicare and Medicaid: Do they accept these programs? You may be using private insurance or funds when you start, but will you have to move if you eventually use Medicaid?

❖ Cost: Get a copy of their fee schedule. What is included in their basic fee? What is extra?

❖ Culture: Spend some time there to determine if the environment is consistent with your beliefs and values.

❖ Special Needs: Do they have special facilities for certain diseases such as Alzheimer's?

Nursing Home Checklists

Checklists are available to help you evaluate the quality of a nursing home. The Health Care Financing Administration Publication No. HCFA-02174 is very helpful. Order it at www.medicare.gov or by calling 1-800-633-4227.

By doing this before you need to, you will retain a tremendous amount of control over where you end up, if you end up using this type of facility. You will also gain some insight into the type of care that elderly people require and you can begin to design a way to have that same care in your own home. Once you come up with a plan, communicate it to that person who will be making the arrangements if you are too sick to do it yourself.

The Bottom Line

It is never easy losing your independence, but you can take some steps now to ensure that your needs and desires are met during this phase of your life.

All the cousins were gathered around the big four-poster bed. They had all loved their grandmother dearly. She had lived through hard times but had always managed to keep her dignity and her sense of humor.

Sarah was by herself in her later years but was always cooking for the church social, the shut-ins down the street, or the pack of grand-kids visiting that weekend. Her home actually belonged to one of her sons, who had purchased it for her to retire in. Her husband had died an early death, leaving very little in the way of assets. She got by on a very small pension and never would admit that she needed money but when her children visited, they would hide tens and twenties in her coat pockets, her desk drawers, and the cookie jar so she would find it and think she'd left it there. If they tried to hand it to her, she wouldn't accept it.

Two days ago, when she died, the family knew that she would be buried in the plot next to her husband that they purchased when he died 25 years ago. They knew that they would all chip in for the funeral expenses. As her friends and neighbors gathered with her family for her funeral, it was a beautiful day and a lovely event. There was food everywhere they turned and flowers on every table. Most of her grandchildren were married with children of their own and they had all grown up sharing the love of Sarah.

Her antique desk, her bed, her wedding ring, and a gold-plated van-ity set were all that she had left of any value. And now that the funeral was over, they all gathered around her bed to do the impor-tant work of dividing up her estate. Tension was high and anger flared because, you see, there were 22 of them and only four things they cared about. To them their grandma was rich. She was rich with the wisdom of her years, the beauty of her spirit, and the depth of her love. They hadn't noticed that this wealth didn't translate into material things until today. They all wanted something tangible to carry with them to continue her presence in their lives.

But, she knew her family better than they knew themselves and when the will was read, she told them that she knew she couldn't make them all happy; and that to make one of them happy at the expense of the others was something that she couldn't do. So, she left every-thing she had to her church and instructed them to take whatever money they could get and buy new playground equipment because, she explained, her greatest joy throughout her life was watching her children play.

Chapter 15

The Final Chapter

Planning what happens to your estate when you die is something you can do right now, get it over with, and go on living a wonderful life. But it's hard to think about and even harder for your heirs to deal with if you don't think about it.

Estate Planning

Estate is just a fancy way to say "stuff." But, more specifically it's the stuff that you haven't lost, had stolen, or had a grandkid break by the time you die. Stuff doesn't necessarily have to have any value. Sometimes it takes up space, sometimes it's just a piece of paper representing value in something, like a stock or a bond, sometimes it's a chunk of land, or a piece of a family business. The old saying, "You can't take it with you," really implies that it just won't fit in that coffin. If you have accumulated what most of us are working on accumulating, there's just an awful lot of it and the fact is that somebody's got to do something with it.

I've been to hundreds of auctions in my short life and it's absolutely amazing the kind of stuff that people hold on to. I find myself wondering sometimes if people knew what they had and really intended to keep it. Or if they just forgot about it when they put it away and never bothered to open that closet again. Antique dealers thrive on the stuff that people forget for a long time and then seek out buyers who find value in it.

So, estate planning is really stuff planning. The more stuff planning you do before you die the less your heirs have to do after you die. It's just a really polite thing to do. Since we haven't gotten real comfortable in our society talking about the eventuality of death, you'll often hear people trying to adjust that reality by asking if someone has a will. If someone asks you this someday, it might be a clue that they think you're going to die (or get separated from your stuff) soon.

Well, the answer in 100 percent of the cases is, yes. You have a will. What they really want to know is whether you have a will that *you* wrote because, you see, the state writes a will for all of us. You have the option to write a will that trumps the will that the state has ready for us. You may not like the way the state's will divides up your stuff for you.

When I was an insurance agent, in the late '70s, estate taxes were a major reason to purchase life insurance. Essentially what the Federal Government did was take the value of your stuff and scrape off a portion of it before you were able to give it to your heirs. This caused a lot of trauma to people with stuff that wasn't easily scraped, like a family business or a family farm. So, life insurance cash was an easy solution to pay those taxes and keep the business or the farm in once piece. Thanks to the tax law changes since then most of us will have no fear of estate taxes during this lifetime.

Treatment of Retirement Benefits

Your retirement benefits will go to the person you named as your beneficiary. They will receive the balance at the time of your death.

So, back to the planning problem—you're sitting there and you've got all this stuff. Some of it has value. Some of it is easily marketable. Some of it has value but isn't easily marketable, like Uncle Joe's grand piano that's going to take eight women to move it and you're not quite sure who's going to pay you money for it. Other stuff has value to you and your family but might not be worth 10 cents to anyone outside the family. And then other items are common household things that might bring a few dollars at an auction but could be useful to someone in the family, if they happen to need one of those items.

Even though you'll be dead when all of this happens, you do have an awful lot of control over it. For instance, you can give away a lot of it before you die. You can tag things and say, "Susie gets this and Johnny gets that." You can determine that everything will be sold at auction and all of your heirs can come and bid against the general public, or you can determine that a private auction would be easier and your kids just bid against each other. Probably the worst option is to let your heirs figure it out themselves because, necessarily, they will be upset and grieving after your death. This is not a good time to test their superior interpersonal skills and negotiation talents. You have the control to play favorites or disinherit them all if you like. It's your stuff and they don't have any right to it unless you give it to them or unless you die without your own will and the state gives it to them.

There is a system we have set up through our courts to allow your will and other documents you create to be handled by impartial arbiters like attorneys and judges and trustees and guardians. This process is called, in many states, the probate process and the court that manages it is called the probate court. In recent years there's been a lot written about how to avoid probate like it's something evil. It may not be evil but it is sometimes expensive, oftentimes complicated, and usually takes some time. So, avoiding probate may work for you and your heirs very well, but in other situations probate may be exactly what you need in order to make sure your wishes are carried out.

Public Nature of Probate

Wills that pass through probate become a matter of public record that anyone can read. Your heirs may not want their private information available to anyone to read.

Let me give you an example. Let's say you have a CD worth $100,000 and you go into the bank and you fill out a Payable on Death order that directs that bank to split that between your two children. So, on your death, $50,000 would go to one child (or half, whatever the balance is at that point) and the other half would go to the other child. But let's say that instead of your children you would like to distribute it equally among your grandchildren and you would like to not have to go back and fill out a new card each time a new grandchild is born. This would be an easier situation to handle through probate because in your will you could direct that that asset be distributed equally among all living grandchildren. You could even instruct that if the grandchild has died but has children that are living that it could then be passed on down to them. So, you can see you have a lot more flexibility using a document that a lawyer would draw up for you than a document that's already been prepared and is standardized for a particular use by a financial institution.

Your life insurance proceeds do not pass through the probate process unless you name your estate as your beneficiary. This is something that you can do if you then want your estate to manage the distribution of the life insurance benefit. But, as we talked about in chapter nine, the insurance company can be very flexible also with your beneficiary designation. If you've never handled someone else's estate after their death, you would have no idea how complicated it can get. One of the nicest things you can do for your family is to simplify it as much as possible by taking deliberate proactive steps to make things clear and systematic as they take care of getting rid of your stuff.

Final Decisions

If you've hung around funerals much in the last few years, you'll notice that there's a phrase that comes up more often than not: "It's what she would have wanted." But there's an element of guessing in the phrase. It implies that people don't really know what she wanted or else they would have said, "It's what she said she wanted." An important part of grieving is to continue to honor the deceased person's wishes, to pay respect to their life and continuing life in your heart.

Once again, this becomes much easier if your wishes are clear and documented and easy to follow. In our state, there's now an indication on our driver's licenses whether we intend to have our organs donated for transplant. It can say clear as day on our driver's license that this is what we wanted; however, I'm told by medical professionals that if the family objects, then it probably isn't going to happen. You're dead, after all, and can't argue about it anymore. This is a wonderful example of how important it is to communicate your wishes to those close around you who will be making key decisions at the end of your life. It's not enough for you to know what you want, you have to tell others what you want and it's helpful to tell your attorney what you want because she may have more power at her disposal to make it happen.

Many funeral homes provide extensive counseling services to help walk you through the various decisions that your family will be asked to make. These choices can stay on file with them until they're needed. This takes a tremendous amount of pressure off of your loved ones at a time when they're not in the best shape to be making these decisions. You also have the option with most funeral homes to begin payment or make full prepayment on those arrangements. You learned in Chapter 6, "Putting Together Your Plan," how to decide whether that is a good use of your money or not. You can calculate the present value of the total cost of funeral expenses at an interest rate that you might earn on that money if you invested it elsewhere and you can determine if the discount that the funeral home is offering you is worth it to you. A good reason to do this is to make sure that the funeral is paid for and a family member doesn't have to come up with cash immediately upon your death, possibly going into debt or selling an asset at a time that isn't advantageous.

Make your decisions and then talk them over with the family members that would most likely be dealing with the funeral home at your death. And, by the way, while you're at it if you still have older family members living, this is a good time to walk them through the process as well and get to know their wishes completely.

Legal Documents

Living Wills

The newest kids on the block are documents many times referred to as a Living Will and a Durable Health Power of Attorney. Different states have different laws governing these documents. You should consult with an attorney, or your local library, to see what's common. The general idea behind them is that many people will not want to be kept alive through artificial means beyond when they would have a meaningful life. Usually at this point they are not competent or conscious and therefore can't direct their own care. This leaves the doctors and family members to make a very difficult decision. One of these documents can direct, for you, instructions that the doctors and family members can follow without fear of going against your wishes or violating any laws.

The same problem holds with these documents, though, as with any of your final wishes. If you haven't communicated to your family that a) they exist and b) it's really what you want, you may not have your wishes carried out. In some places you can actually record these documents, just like you can record a will, with your county government. This allows the documents to be public and allows hospitals access to the documents at a time when they may need to see them. Again the problem is, they need to know there's a document that they're looking for and generally someone needs to tell them that. It wouldn't be uncommon for your family physician to know that you have signed one of these documents. But, when you arrive at the emergency room the resident treating you will not have the time to look back through pages and pages of charts or to call your family physician to ask the question. So, once you determine whether this type of document is something you'd like to have, it's important that you get it completed (sooner than later), you communicate it well to people close to you, and you keep it in a place where it can be found or record it with a public office.

Last Will and Testament

The most obvious document that you need before you die is your will. A will is a personal document—there is no such thing as a joint will. You will have one and you may write it many times before you die. You can add and subtract things from it. You can say lots of different things in it. And you have some options as to where to keep it. You've probably heard the advice that you don't want to keep it in your Safe Deposit Box because that gets sealed on your death.

There are some differing opinions as to how to write a will. Obviously, the attorneys in the country would advise that you use a member of their profession and they do these very routinely, very often, usually for fairly low flat rates. There are also do-it-yourself will kits, which can apply to some circumstances very well and might actually complicate other circumstances. Once you realize that you already have a will, that the state has written one for you under the laws of intestate (dying intestate means dying without your own will) the standard will that they've written may not be at all what you would prefer to do with your stuff. So that should scare you a little into at least filling out a will from a will kit until you can make an appointment and save the money to pay for an attorney's advice. If you already have a will, it's a really good idea to read it now and then and make sure that your wishes at the time it was written are the same as your wishes now. Wills can be easily changed and the new version overrides the old version.

Trusts

Another legal document that's important to consider is a Trust. There are several different types of Trust that help in planning your estate. Probably the most common is a Testamentary Trust, which just means that it doesn't exist until you die. There's a piece of paper that creates it, but it won't have any money and it won't do anything unless you're dead. So, there are no fees for managing, no tax returns to file, no additional work to manage your finances. A Testamentary Trust is a wonderful tool to be able to leave money to children. You can direct your will or your life insurance policies or your payable-on-death accounts to direct your money to a trust set up for the benefit of your minor heirs. What this does is immediately place the management of those assets in the hands of a trustee whom you name. That trustee can be an attorney, a bank (trust department), relative, or friend. That trustee can continue to manage your money and provide support for those children in the same way that you would have. If it's important to you that that child attends college, you can direct the trustee to pay out monies for college tuition for the child.

If you instead leave the money directly to the child, a guardian would be appointed by the court to manage the money on behalf of the child until the child is 18, at which point the Court would direct the guardian to deliver the money to the child. I don't know what you were up to at 18, but my guess is that any amount of a windfall would have been spent before you could say "Cancun."

These decisions, that will make life easier for those who continue living past your death, are not as complicated as they are emotional. They bring up all of the fear and sadness and anxiety surrounding your own death. It's been my experience with my clients that if we can work through these decisions, get them on paper, get them filed appropriately, and then put them away, life becomes a little less pressured. You really only have to do it once, unless things change drastically in your situation. If you think of it as a gift, as opposed to a burden, it can turn into a very loving experience.

The Bottom Line

Check these items off your life's To Do List as soon as possible. They are emotional but terribly important. Your family will be able to return to a normal life much more quickly if you have done your planning well.

Congratulations! Wow! You made it. A couple of hundred pages ago I had my doubts. I saw your eyes roll the first time you had to get out your calculator for real and I heard all the curse words you know when we got to that stuff on present value. You got mad at the government a bunch of times and mad at me a few times. You met some very intriguing women and saw a very personal side of their lives.

But, more than anything, you got to know yourself. You thought about things that you'd never considered before. You wrestled with some demons that you didn't know were still there, and you discovered that you are a good problem solver, especially when you can define the problem well.

This is the end of the book but this is not the end of your job. You have many wonderful years ahead of you and lots of things will change, but each time they do I hope you'll take with you some of the strategies and skills and strengths that you've acquired through your hard work and careful planning.

I want to thank you for the opportunity to share my thoughts with you and tell you that it's been pure joy to be a part of your life-planning process. I hope you'll write and tell me what has changed for you and what you're looking forward to in your retirement.

edie.milligan@paydayplanning.com

Glossary

accrue   To increase. When interest accrues on your loan, it accumulates according to the current interest rate for that loan and the amount you owe.

adjustable rate mortgages (ARMs)   A mortgage for a fixed amount of debt, for a fixed period of time, with a variable rate of interest. ARMs typically have a maximum annual increase limit of 2 percent and an overall cap on total interest rate increase of 6 percent.

adjusted balance method   The best approach for calculating the monthly finance charge on a credit card from the point of view of the consumer. The finance charge is based on the amount you owe, after all payments are applied to your balance.

amortization   The process of repaying an obligation, such as a mortgage, over a period of time. Part of each payment is used to pay the current interest owed, the remainder going to reduce the principle.

annual percentage rate (APR)   In terms of mortgages, the APR includes all points paid and interest paid over the life of the loan. For variable rate mortgages, this rate will change as the interest rate changes.

annual renewable term (ART)   Life insurance that runs for one year and then renews without evidence of insurability, usually with a slightly higher premium.

annuity   Contract with an insurance company that guarantees a regular payout for the life of the annuitant.

ARMs   *See* adjustable rate mortgages.

asset allocation   System of choosing investment types based on their proportionate representation in a portfolio of investments.

assets   Any possession that could be sold or exchanged for value or is generating income.

automatic income reinvestment   A feature of some investments that purchases more of the same investment using the dividend or interest paid by the investment.

average daily balance   Outstanding daily balance of a line of credit, divided by the number of days in the billing period.

average daily balance method   The next best and most commonly used approach to calculating the monthly finance charge on a credit card from the consumer's point of view. Interest is charged based on the "average daily balance" of the account over the course of the billing period.

average tax rate   The percentage of total taxable income paid to a government in taxes.

balance sheet   A financial statement that provides a snapshot of a person's or business's financial position. It subtracts liabilities from assets to arrive at net worth.

balloon mortgages   A mortgage with a fixed amount of debt and a fixed or variable rate of interest. Typically, payment is made for a fixed period of time, after which the entire loan comes due.

basis   The value assigned to an investment at its acquistion. Also known as cost basis.

benefit period   The length of time that a disability insurance policy would provide income in the event of disability. Stated either in weeks, months, years, or to a certain age.

bridge loan   A short-term loan, usually six months to one year in term, designed to provide funds for a short period of time, payable in full at the end of the period. Usually incurred in anticipation of a future event, such as the sale of a home or other asset, or the anticipated receipt of future income.

capital gain   The amount of money earned on an investment derived from its increase in value from the date of purchase to the date of sale.

capitalize   As used in reference to indebtedness, to add unpaid accrued interest to unpaid principal. This increases your total outstanding principal. Thus, if you choose a lender that capitalizes once a year or more, you may be paying interest on interest. As used in reference to investing, to use or convert to capital; to establish the stock of a new business at a certain price; to supply capital to a business; to use something to one's advantage.

cash advance   A withdrawal of cash from a credit card, usually from an ATM, which results in an unsecured debt. Many cards charge a minimum fee at the time the advance is made in addition to charging interest from the date of the advance.

cash flow statement   A financial statement that provides detailed information about income and expenses over a period of time.

cash value life insurance   A permanent life insurance contract that accumulates an amount of money that can be borrowed or cash out.

certificate of deposit (CD)   A savings instrument typically issued by a bank that pays a fixed rate of interest for a known period of time. Maturities range from several weeks to several years.

coinsurance   The sharing of a potential risk between the insured and the insurance company. A common feature of health insurance policies, this provision requires that the insured pay a percentage of the loss up to the maximum "stop loss limit" following the payment of a deductible. *See also* stop loss provision.

collateral   An asset that is pledged as security against the default of a loan.

compound interest   Interest that is paid or received on interest from prior periods. *See also* simple interest.

consolidation   A method of combining several loans into a single loan with an extended repayment term of up to 30 years. This can be an effective method of lowering your monthly payment.

consumer debt   Nonmortgage debt that is used to fund consumer-related purchases; common examples include auto loans and revolving debt used to purchase other personal use goods.

co-sign   To take on the responsibility for debt repayment along with the person assuming the primary responsibility for loan repayment. In the event of default on the loan by the primary debtor, full responsibility for repayment of the debt falls to the co-signer.

credit card   A piece of plastic with which one can incur unsecured consumer debt on a revolving account with a lender.

credit collection agency   A business involved in the collection of debt for a third party.

credit limit   Maximum available credit on a given line of credit or credit card.

credit score   Rating of an individual's creditworthiness as defined by a formula. Used by lenders to evaluate the risk involved in extending credit or offering a loan to an individual or business.

current assets   Readily accessible assets that are held as cash or can be easily converted to cash. Liquid assets such as cash, or money held in a checking or savings account or money market fund or account.

current liabilities   Debts that are due within a short period of time, typically one to six months.

decreasing term insurance   Temporary life insurance contract where the premium remains level and the face value (death benefit) reduces over time. Often used to fund mortgage payoffs.

debit card   The electronic equivalent of a check, which automatically withdraws money (debits) from your checking or savings account.

debt   An obligation or liability.

debtor   A person who incurs a liability or debt; the one who is obligated to repay a debt.

deductible   The amount the insured must pay in the event of a loss before coverage is provided by the policy. The deductible amount is always stated in the policy.

default   Failure to repay a loan. This will negatively affect your credit rating for up to seven years.

default risk   The probability that a borrower or bond issuer will not repay the principle of the debt.

deferment   A time when you are not required to make payments. During the deferment, interest continues to accrue on the loan. Deferments may be granted for reasons such as half-time study, unemployment, economic hardship, graduate fellowships, and rehabilitation training.

deferred annuities   An annuity contract where the regular payments to the annuitant begin a year or more after the premium is paid.

deficit spending   Spending that exceeds income over a given period of time.

defined benefit pension plan   A retirement savings plan that qualifies for an income tax deferral on the contributions. Funded by the employer, it provides a benefit based on income and years of service. Contributions to the plan are calculated to arrive at a specifically "defined benefit."

defined contribution pension plan   A retirement savings plan that qualifies for an income tax deferral on the contributions. Funded by the employer, it provides a variable benefit based upon the earnings of the fund. Contributions to the plan are calculated as a percentage of income.

delinquency   Failure to make a loan payment when it is due. If you are more than 90 days delinquent, your delinquency will be reported to the national credit bureaus and will negatively affect your credit rating. If you are delinquent for 180 days or more, you are considered in default.

disability income insurance   A contract with an insurance company that provides monthly benefits in the event of a loss of income due to physical or mental disability.

disbursement   The date a loan check is issued by the lender. Some lenders issue loan funds electronically.

diversification   The practice of selecting a variety of investments to include in a portfolio. Characteristics might include maturity date, size of investment, inherent risk, type of investment, and tax treatment of investment.

dividends   Proportionate shares of earnings of a corporation voluntarily paid out to holders of common and preferred shares of stock.

dollar-cost averaging   A system of purchasing investments that buys the same dollar amount of the investment on the same day each month, regardless of the underlying value of the investment.

down payment   The initial deposit required when financing a purchase; the amount "put down" at time of purchase; a portion of the full purchase price. The size of the down payment can affect the number of "points" charged or the interest rate charged on a loan.

durable power of attorney   A legal document that appoints another to control an individual's affairs should the individual become mentally or physically incapacitated.

earnings per share (EPS)   The amount of profit a company earned divided by the number of outstanding common shares of stock. This may or may not be paid out in a dividend at the discretion of the board of directors.

elimination period   A disability insurance contract provision that stipulates the period of time between the onset of a covered disability and the date that the payment of benefits begin under the terms of the policy. *See also* waiting period.

equity   The difference between the value of an asset and any amount borrowed to fund that asset.

estate planning   The process of determining how your assets and liabilities will be handled at your death. Involves both financial and legal strategies.

federal gift and estate tax   Taxes levied on assets passed to others before (gift) and after (estate) death. Many exclusions make it a rare tax that few individuals pay.

Federal Housing Administration (FHA)   FHA loans are available to qualifying individuals and families and carry slightly lower interest rates than are commercially available—with lower requirements for down payments as well. FHA charges you an upfront premium for 30 years worth of FHA mortgage insurance, part of which will be returned to the buyer who pays the loan in full over the life of the loan.

financial risk   The probability that the investment will not be able to pay a return to the investor.

first mortgage   The primary debt position against real property.

fixed income   A type of investment that pays a stated return, such as a bond with a contractual coupon rate.

fixed-rate mortgage   A loan collateralized by real property—for a fixed amount of debt, for a fixed period of time, at a fixed rate of interest, with a fixed payment.

foreclosure   To call for the full payment of debt prior to full term of the loan—usually due to default of loan payments past due.

front end load   A sales fee paid by an investor when purchasing an investment.

fund family   A group of mutual funds managed by the same investment management company.

future value   The anticipated value of a present amount or stream of payments, assuming a given rate of inflation and return on investment, over a given period of time.

grace period   For credit cards, a period of time during which no interest is payable—only if the balance is paid in full on or before the due date of the prior statement period. If the balance is not paid in full on or before the due date of the payment, interest is charged from the original date of purchase, with no grace period. Cash advances have no grace period. For insurance policies, a contract provision that requires a period of "grace" during which insurance remains in force without premium payment, in anticipation of payment. This contract provision prevents policy cancellation for a period of time, as defined in the policy contract, beyond the "premium due date."

graduated payment mortgages (GPMs)   A mortgage with a fixed amount of debt for a fixed period of years, with a fixed or variable interest rate, with a payment that starts low and gradually increases over the life of the loan. In the early years, the payment is usually not enough to cover interest charges, resulting in increased debt and increased total interest charges over the life of the loan.

growth and income fund   A mutual fund that invests in both strong companies known to pay regular dividends and less established companies with growth potential.

guaranteed renewable   A term usually used in reference to a health insurance, disability insurance, or long-term care insurance policy. This contract provision states that the policy cannot be cancelled as long as premiums are paid in a timely manner. Premiums are not guaranteed to remain unchanged, however. If premiums are raised, the increase must apply to an entire group as opposed to individual selection.

health maintenance organization (HMO)   A health plan that collects premiums in advance to provide a wide range of services from a specific panel of providers.

home equity line of credit (HELOC)   A flexible line of credit against the accumulated equity of a residence, typically a second mortgage, with a variable interest rate charged on the outstanding credit balance only. Interest is generally charged on the average daily balance. Minimum payment due is sometimes interest only, or interest plus 1 to 2 percent of the outstanding balance. Payments in excess of the required minimum can (and should) be made at any time without prepayment penalty.

home equity (HE) loan   A fixed loan against the accumulated equity of a residence, typically a second mortgage, usually for a fixed period of time (typically 1 to 10 years) at a fixed rate of interest with a fixed monthly payment. HE loans can also be variable rate loans. *See also* home equity line of credit (HELOC).

homeowner's insurance   A contract of insurance that protects the named insured from loss as the result of physical damage to a principal residence. Liability protection is also frequently provided which protects the homeowner and dependents from claims for personal injury caused by the named insured.

indexing   The practice of automatically increasing something, such as a tax rate, based upon some other measurement, such as the inflation rate.

Individual Retirement Account (IRA)   Tax status given to an investment that allows a deferral of income taxes paid on the contribution and its earnings until withdrawn.

inflation   A general decrease in the value of money. Commonly reported as the Consumer Price Index (CPI).

inflation risk   The probability that a decrease in the value of money will erode the earnings on a fixed income investment.

insurable interest   The stake one has in another's continued existance. If a beneficiary holds an insurable interest in the insured, life insurance proceeds are not taxable.

interest   For debt, money you must pay for the "privilege" of borrowing money, expressed as a percentage of the outstanding principal. For fixed income investments, the yield or return on an investment. Income received as a result of lending money.

interest rate risk   The probability that changes in interest rates will affect the value of an asset in the future.

intestate   The condition of dying without a will.

investment assets   Assets that are held by an individual or business with an expectation of return of income or growth of principal. Not a personal use asset.

Keogh plan (HR10)   A tax advantaged retirement savings plan available to self-employed individuals.

landlord's insurance   Property and casualty insurance that provides protection to a landlord in the event of property or casualty loss.

late payment fee   A charge that is levied for late payment of a minimum balance due on a line of credit or credit card. This charge is added to the prior balance due.

lessee   The user of a leased asset that pays the lessor for the right to use the asset.

lessor   The owner of a leased asset who receives income for allowing another party use of the asset.

leverage   The use of debt to purchase assets.

liability   An obligation to pay, a responsibility.

liability insurance   Commercial insurance that provides for protection against the potential financial loss for the insured in the event the insured was found responsible for injury or damages to another party.

line of credit   An agreement by a lender to loan money to a customer, on an "as needed" basis, up to a certain amount at a predetermined rate of interest.

liquidity   The relative amount of time it takes to turn an asset into cash. The shorter the time, the more liquid the investment.

living will   A legal document instructing doctors on your care should you become unable to communication your wishes.

loan   A debt issue, typically due within 1 to 10 years.

managed care   A practice developed by health insurance companies to control costs and enhance the quality of health care paid for by the benefits under their policies.

management fee   The price an investor pays to an asset management company for their services. Usually stated in a yearly percentage of assets under management.

marginal tax rate   Stated as a percentage, the amount of income tax that would be paid on the next dollar earned.

market volatility risk   The probability that the value of an investment will be affected by the normal cycles of its market.

marketability risk   The probability that an investment will lose value due to a lack of ability to sell it in the future.

maturity date   The date on which a financial contract becomes due, as in the case of a loan, CD, or bond instrument.

Medicaid   A government program designed to pay the health care and long term care costs for impoverished individuals.

Medicare   A government program that collects premiums from workers through their payroll and pays for the medical care costs of individuals over 65 and some disabled individuals under 65.

minimum payment   The minimum amount due on an outstanding balance of a loan, typically represents interest charges for the period plus 1 to 2 percent of the outstanding balance.

minimum payment due   The absolute minimum that must be paid on a line of credit or credit card to avoid default.

money market mutual fund   A managed group of short-term debt instruments paying a stated interest rate.

mortgage   Debt using real property as collateral, typically for a fixed period of time, for a fixed or variable rate of interest. The pledging of real property to a creditor against the potential default of a loan.

mortgage lender   The mortgagor. The person or entity offering the loan to the mortgagee, with real property held as collateral.

mortgage point   *See* point.

mortgagee   The debtor. The individual or entity assuming a liability that is collateralized by real property.

mutual fund   A diversified portfolio of securities owned by an investment company that allows smaller investors to buy shares of the combined portfolio.

net asset value   The value of each share of a mutual fund. Calculated by taking the total value of the fund and dividing it by the number of outstanding shares.

net worth statement   A measure of value. Total assets minus total liabilities equals net worth. Also called balance sheet.

no-load mutual fund   A mutual fund with no sales fee at the time of purchase.

nonprobate property   Assets owned at death that pass directly to a beneficiary without going through the instructions in a will. Includes Payable-on-Death accounts, life insurance, trust assets, and joint with right of survivorship assets.

opportunity cost   The income lost from placing money in a different investment.

out-of-pocket cost   Maximum cost that can be incurred by the insured in the event of a loss. *See also* stop loss provision.

overinsured   To have insurance protection in excess of the potential value of loss as the result of a covered risk.

past due balance   Indicates that a prior payment has not been made before the payment due date. Past due balances must be paid in full to avoid possible foreclosure of the debt.

permanent insurance   Life insurance that is intended to cover the risk of loss of life for the insured's full life. Usually features a level premium and a build up of a cash value inside the contract.

personal use assets   Assets owned by an individual for their personal use or enjoyment.

point   For debt, typically, 1 percent of the loan amount. Points are considered "prepaid interest" and as such are income tax deductible. Points paid on the principal mortgage are deductible the year paid; points paid upon refinance are deductible over the life of the loan. For investing, typically a unit value of $1.00 used for quoting changes in stock prices. A bond point is equal to $10 (1 percent of $1000 face value).

portability   A feature of many employee benefits, such as pension plans and life insurance, that allows an employee to carry the coverage with them as they leave the company.

preexisting condition   A condition that existed prior to the issuance of insurance.

preferred provider organization (PPO)   A group of medical care providers that contract with an insurance company to provide services at a reduced rate.

premium   Price. As used in insurance, the cost of insurance coverage for a stipulated period of time. As used in investments, trading at a price in excess of par.

present value   The current value of a future amount, or stream of payments, assuming a given rate of inflation and return on investment over a given period of time.

previous balance method   The worst method for determining the finance charge on a credit card from the point of view of the consumer. Interest is charged on the previous statement balance, as if no payments were made during the billing period.

price/earnings ratio (P/E ratio)   The Price of a share of stock divided into the Earnings per share (EPS).

principal   The full amount borrowed, or the balance of the loan that has not yet been repaid. This may include capitalized interest. Interest is calculated as a percentage of this amount.

probate   The legal process that ensures that the debts and assets of a deceased individual are handled according to the law and all legal documents that were prepared.

profit-sharing plan   A defined contribution type of qualified pension plan that allows contributions based upon the profit level of the employer.

promissory note   A contract with the lender that you, the borrower, sign before the loan is disbursed. This contract states that you will repay the loan and legally binds you to its terms and conditions.

qualified pension plan   A plan approved by the IRS to qualify for deferred tax status. It must not discriminate.

quarters of coverage   A system used by the Social Security Administration to determine eligibility for benefits. Based on the amount of earnings in a calendar year. Forty quarters allows a worker to qualify for retirement benefits.

real income   Income adjusted for inflation.

real property   An asset that consists of land or buildings.

real return on investment   The earnings adjusted for inflation.

refinance   To restructure a debt or mortgage, typically to take advantage of reduced interest rates, to reduce payments, or to consolidate debt into one line of credit.

repayment schedule   In reference to student loans, a document received shortly after leaving school that states the loan principal, the monthly payment amount, and provides a schedule of dates when payments are due.

return   Income, dividends, capital gain, interest, or any other revenue received because of ownership of an asset.

revolving credit   A legal commitment by a bank or other lending institution to loan money to a customer as needed up to a stated maximum limit, for a stipulated period of time, which may extend for a number of years.

risk management   The process of avoiding, reducing, eliminating, sharing, or insuring financial risk using various methods and strategies.

rollover IRA   An Individual Retirement Account funded with money from a pension fund already tax-deferred.

rule of 72   By dividing the interest rate into 72, the result shows how many years it will take principle to double at that rate. For example, a 6 percent investment will double in 12 years.

second mortgage   A secondary debt position against real property.

secondary market   In lending, a company that buys loans from lenders. Lenders often sell loans to secondary markets so that they can continually replenish their lending funds, which in turn get marketed to fixed income investors. In investing, the purchase or sale of an investment that takes place after the primary offering.

settlement options   The choices available to the beneficiary of a life insurance death benefit which include lump sum, life annuity, and period certain.

secured credit card   A consumer credit card that is secured by deposits in a bank or other financial institution.

secured debt   Debt that is secured by collateral.

self-insured   An individual or business with sufficient assets to meet a potential financial loss from a known risk.

simple interest   When interest is calculated using a "simple method," interest is calculated at the end of the period. To calculate the interest earned on $1000 earning 6 percent in a year, simply multiply $1,000 by .06. The result is $60 interest earnings per year of "simple interest." *See also* compound interest.

Social Security statement   A yearly report sent out from the Social Security Administration providing all earnings and benefit estimates.

stop loss provision   An insurance term that defines the maximum loss potential of the insured. For example, a health insurance stop loss provision limits the maximum annual out-of-pocket cost to the insured to $1,500 (the stated annual deductible of $500 plus $1,000 or 20 percent of the co-insurance limit of $5,000).

Student Aid Report (SAR)   Received a couple of weeks after the Free Application for Federal Student Aid (FAFSA) is mailed to the processor. The SAR contains all the information provided on the FAFSA, messages from the processor, and some calculations. Upon receipt, the SAR should be reviewed to make sure that all of the information is correct.

subordinated debt   Debt that is in a lesser position in terms of security of principal. In the event of bankruptcy or liquidation, subordinated debt holders are paid after secured debtors. For example, a second mortgage is subordinate to the principal mortgage on a home.

subsidized loans   A loan that is supported by the lender or third party such as the Veterans Administration (VA) or the Small Business Administration (SBA). (For example, the Stafford student loan is a subsidized loan. The U.S. government pays the interest on this loan for you while you are in school, during your six-month grace period, and during periods of authorized deferment.)

surrender charge   Also known as a "Contingent Deferred Charge" (CDSC). Typically, this is a reducing charge over a limited period of years. The charge imposed by the insurance company upon termination or surrender of a life insurance contract or annuity. The sales charge imposed upon the surrender of "B" or "C" shares of mutual funds.

surrender value   The amount payable in cash value available to the policy owner upon voluntary termination of a cash value life insurance contract. Policy surrender value equals cash value less surrender charges, if any, imposed by the contracts.

T-bill   A type of simple interest U.S. government security that matures (comes due) in one year or less. Available maturities are 13-week, 26-week, or 52-week. Interest payments on many debt instruments are tied to the T-bill rate. The investors who buy them are making a short-term loan to the federal government.

tax sheltered annuity (TSA)   An annuity contract, which allows an income tax deferral on the deposit to the contract.

tenant's insurance   Property and liability insurance that protects a person who leases property from another.

term   The length of time you have to repay a loan.

term insurance   Life insurance issued for a specified period of time for a specified annual premium. Term insurance does not typically have cash value.

time value of money   The value of money stated in terms of present or future value, taking into account the passage of time and an assumed rate of return and inflation.

umbrella insurance   Personal liability insurance protection that provides insurance beyond the underlying coverage of an individual's auto and homeowners insurance policies.

underinsured   An individual who has insufficient insurance to protect them from the full risk of a potential loss.

underwrite   To choose a risk to insure.

uninsurable   An individual who, because of known conditions, represents a level of risk that an insurance company is not willing to accept.

uninsured   An individual who has no insurance or protection from risk of potential loss.

universal life insurance Flexible cash value life insurance that typically pays a current, competitive rate of interest on cash value accumulations. Universal life offers a variety of options that result in a flexible product design. At the policy owner's discretion, premium mode and amount can vary as well as death benefit options. Policy loans of cash value are available at an interest rate stipulated in the insurance contract. Partial withdrawals of cash value are also available.

unsecured debt Debt that is issued without collateral.

unsubsidized loans A loan that is not supported in any way by a federal agency or other third party. One example is one type of Stafford loan. This type of loan accrues (accumulates) interest while a student is in school, during the six-month grace period after leaving school, and during any authorized periods of deferment and forbearance. *See also* subsidized loans.

U.S. Savings Bonds Bonds that are issued by the U.S. Department of the Treasury and backed by the full faith and credit of the U.S. Government.

U.S. Treasury Securities Any debt instrument issued by the U.S. government. These include Treasury Bills, notes, and bonds. The interest rates for federal (and many private) student loans are based on the results of Treasury Bill auctions held throughout the year by the U.S. government. Treasury Bills and other "securities" are sold to the public to pay off maturing government debt and to raise the cash needed to operate the federal government. *See also* T-bill.

variable annuity An annuity contract that invests its deposits in equity investments.

variable universal life insurance Flexible cash value life insurance that offers a number of investment account options in addition to the other features of a universal life policy. *See also* universal life insurance.

vesting The schedule used by qualified pension plans to determine how quickly a participant owns the deposits made by their employer on their behalf.

Veteran's Administration (VA) loans VA mortgage loans are available to qualifying individuals and families and carry slightly lower interest rates than are commercially available, with lower requirements for downpayments as well.

waiting period   Period of time between the onset of disability and the payment of benefits under the terms of the policy. Also known as elimination period.

waiver of premium   An insurance policy rider that waives the required premium payment in the event of an extended period of disability.

whole life insurance   A fixed life insurance policy for the life of the insured. Premiums are usually level and cash values usually increase.

will   A legal document that establishes an individual's instructions for the distribution of their estate assets.

Index

Symbols

401(k)
  analyzing for retirement
    planning, 58-60
  maximum contributions, 60
  types of mutual funds, 59-
    60

A

Accredited Financial
  Counselor. *See* AFC
accumulations, capital, 20-21
action plans (transition), 153
AFC (Accredited Financial
  Counselor), 6
AFCPE (Association for
  Financial Counseling and
  Planning Education), 6
after-tax investments,
  169-170
agents (insurance agents),
  62-63, 66
AHC (Accredited Housing
  Counselor), 6
Alzheimer's disease, 156
American Psychological
  Association Web site, 156
analyzing financial products
  banks, 66-67
  benefit departments, 55-62
    401(k), 58-60

comparing products,
  56-57
IRAs, 61-62
portability of plans, 62
sharing costs, 57-58
insurance issues
  agents, 62-63, 66
  standard product-types,
    64
investment diversification,
  114
stockbrokers, 67
Area Agencies on Aging, 143
asset allocations, 109-111
Association for Financial
  Counseling and Planning
  Education. *See* AFCPE
average tax brackets versus
  marginal, 50-52

B

balancing retirement lifestyles,
  calculations
  bill expenses, 28-29
  debts, 29-31
  expense summaries, 32-37
  frequent expenses, 26-27
  income, 25-26
  out-of-debt dates, 31-32
  payroll deductions, 26
  periodic expenses, 27-28

D

E

F

G

H

U-V

universal life insurance, 64
unsystematic investment risks
    business risks, 112
    default risks, 112
    financial risks, 112

variable annuities, 64

W-Z

whole life insurance, 64
wills
    last will and testament, 201
    living wills, 200-201